PROMISING
WATERS

JIM GRASSI

HARVEST HOUSE PUBLISHERS
Eugene, Oregon 97402

Cover art by Thomas Kinkade, copyright © by Thomas Kinkade, Media Arts Group, Inc. Cover by Left Coast Design, Portland, Oregon.

PROMISING WATERS

Copyright © 1996 by Harvest House Publishers
Eugene, Oregon 97402

Library of Congress Cataloging-in-Publication Data

Grassi, James E., 1943-
    Promising waters / James E. Grassi.
       p.   cm.
    Includes bibliographical references (p.195).
    ISBN 1-56507-499-8   (alk. paper)
    1.   Fishing—Religious aspects—Christianity.   2.   Fishing—
Anecodotes.   3.   Fishers—religious life.   4.   Grassi, James
E., 1943-
      I.   Title.
BV4596.F5G73   1996
248.8'8—dc20   96-10810
                                            CIP

To

Louise—
whose love, faithfulness, and encouragement
have helped sustain me;

Pastor Dan and Thelma Grassi—
for their grace and dedication;

Pastor Tom and Della Grassi—
for their commitment to serve;

Dana Rose and future grandchildren—
may you discover the joys of discipleship;

Dan and Mae Grassi,
Elmer and Bernice Etter-Vindelov—
thank you for providing a godly heritage.

Acknowledgments

I want to express thanks to those who have discipled me. Pastor Chuck Swindoll has periodically provided inspirational counsel and godly advice that helped excite and guide my life and ministry. I am appreciative of James Dobson, Joseph Aldrich, Bill Hull, Bob Coleman, Tim Hansel, Paul Lewis, Bill Butterworth, and Jim Petersen for their insights and encouragement through messages and books. I count it a blessing to have been discipled by my good friends Stan Smith, Gary Chase, Jim Balkcom, Bob Wattles, Sam Beler, Jeff Klippenes, Greg Presnell, and many board members of Let's Go Fishing Ministries. Their efforts and patience have enabled me to catch the vision of what it takes to be a servant-leader.

Thanks also to Bill Jensen, Betty Fletcher, Ron Rhodes, Carolyn McCready, Ed and Mary Belle Steele, and Ed Gobel for their encouragement and support of this work.

A special thanks to Thomas Kinkade, for permission to use "The End of a Perfect Day" as the cover illustration for this book.

Contents

Foreword:
Adventure with a Purpose

We need more men like Jim Grassi. He is a man of contagious vision. He is not only highly skilled in numerous areas of expertise, but also has multifaceted abilities to communicate the deeper truths involved in these activities. Moreover, he is a man who wakes up each morning, thanks God for the incredible gift of life, and then—with the wide-eyed wonder of a child—meets each day as if for the first time.

Jim Grassi's reputation speaks for itself. He is a man who has been successful at virtually everything he has done. In his early career, he was successful in the secular community. Then one day he made the connection between his avid love for fishing and his even more avid love for Jesus Christ. The sparks began to fly, igniting his imagination and creativity. Today, Jim has taken his two magnificent obsessions and melded them into one with astounding results. He founded Let's Go Fishing Ministries!

Jim is a world-class fisherman and I am not. In fact, in conducting a wilderness-survival program associated with my ministry, I think I learned how to catch fish with my bare hands and was better at that than catching them with a pole.

My casts usually warned fish anywhere within a mile to take off because some clunker was out there causing huge waves in what was otherwise a very smooth pond. I think there were occasions when I actually heard the fish laughing along with the two of us. To say I was a klutz would be a generous act of kindness.

Though Jim has been successful at everything he has done in life, it was his life-threatening illness that helped him realize his finiteness. His encounter with Jesus brought him a peace, joy, and power he had never known before through all of his successes.

Jim's life was transformed. As the Russian proverb says, "He who has this disease called Jesus will never be cured." Jim is truly both contagious and infectious, spiritually speaking.

When St. Francis of Assisi said, "Share Jesus always; use words only when necessary," he was giving a preview of men like Jim Grassi, who realized that modeling the Christian life is still the best way to change human behavior. We don't *speak* the message, we *are* the message. I don't know if Jim is aware of it, but Harvard University did a study and found that there are over 700,000 ways to communicate nonverbally. He has been doing this nonverbal communication all along.

What Jim has done, *we all* need to do! He has taken the heart of his passion, combined it with the finest of his skills and gifts, and invested it in the kingdom in an all-or-nothing proposition. Jesus praised people like the widow with the mite (Mark 12:41-44), and the young boy with the loaves and fish (John 6:1-14), not because of how much they gave, but because *they held nothing back.*

In this book you are going to meet a man who holds nothing back in telling you about the One who invented the concept (Jesus). Jim uses a lively writing style combined with a wonderful sense of humor and a natural gift for storytelling. He wants to invite *you* to become a fisher of men.

The best thing, obviously, would be for you to participate in one of Jim's "Let's Go Fishing" experiences. As an old cook in the desert once told me, "God created everything except one thing—and that was a substitute for experience." If you can't do that right now, though, the next best thing is to read this book. Let it hook you! Let it change you so you, in turn, can change others.

That is the essence and purpose of Jim's whole life. And he is one of the best teachers I know at sharing this indescribable adventure with you. But then again, he was taught personally by the Master Himself. He has found the best book on survival and manual for fishing that has ever been written in human history.

Jim wants to invite you to explore that Book—the Bible—and understand why he is so excited about living. He also wants to personally introduce you to its Author. After you have gotten to know Him, you will no doubt find that you cannot help but share Him with the same enthusiasm that leaps off the pages of The Book.

I hope *Promising Waters* sells millions of copies. Jim has put years of effort into it. It is meant to be a guide—a workbook for your own experience—so that you too will not be able to help but share "The Story" that has changed the world.

Get ready for one of the greatest adventures life has to offer!

Years ago, I learned that the word Timothy means "honored by God." Well, I will close by saying that I feel greatly honored to be able not only to introduce this book to you, but to introduce the man, Jim Grassi, to you. Through the combination of the two, I hope you will be introduced to the One who has transformed all of our lives.

— Tim Hansel
President, Summit Expedition
President, Ignite Incorporated

A Personal Note from the Author

Among fishing instructors there is an adage often conveyed to new fishermen: "Ten percent of all fishermen catch 90 percent of the fish."

The successful fisherman properly prepares himself for the challenge. He consistently applies the knowledge and experience that make him an excellent angler (fisherman) every time he goes fishing.

The same is true in discipleship. We need to consistently employ the gifts, talents, and contacts the Lord has provided us to reach others for His kingdom. The twenty-first-century church must be practical and relevant to the world in which we live. Men must be willing to embrace their roles as spiritual leaders and commit themselves to the personal involvement discipleship requires. From the first-century disciples we also learn that effective discipleship requires grace and patience that only God can provide.

German clergyman Dietrich Bonhoeffer informs us that "when we are called to follow Christ, we are summoned to an exclusive attachment to His person.... The call goes forth, and is at once followed by the response of obedience.... Christianity without discipleship is always Christianity without Christ."[1]

Promising Waters is a unique book on practical discipleship designed to capture the imagination and hearts of those with a desire to grow in faith and service. It is specifically directed toward men and is filled with anecdotes, humor, and short stories that express the correlation between fishing and discipleship. It is designed to be both entertaining and easy to read while providing a better understanding of the biblical principles of discipleship.

The call to discipleship is a call to accountability and responsibility for ourselves and others. The apostle Paul was mentored by Barnabas while encouraging the younger Timothy in the things of the Lord. We all need the wisdom and guidance of more mature believers while at the same time developing a relationship with an apprentice eager to learn from what *we* know about God and His Word.

Discipleship requires a receptive attitude and resulting action. Through the study of Christ's relationship with His first-century fishermen-disciples, I pray that you will become a "fisher of men" in spirit and deed.

First Catch

W hen I was five years old, my dad placed a stiff wooden rod and an old reel in my hands. He said, "Son, watch this rod and reel. I'm going to eat some lunch."

My focus was riveted on that line as I waited patiently for the slightest movement. Then, without warning, the rod started jumping around in my hands. The four-pound catfish at the end of that line had no idea that this event would fuel the fires of fascination and excitement that have lasted a lifetime.

Many people probably can't tell you who their first boyfriend or girlfriend was. But almost everyone can tell you *when*, *where*, and *how* they caught their first fish.

Some say fishing is "a jerk on one end of a line waiting for a jerk on the other." Another author defined the sport as "the art of casting, trolling, jigging, or spinning while freezing, sweating, swatting, or swearing." The fact remains, however, that men, women, boys, and girls throughout the ages have immensely enjoyed this marvelous sport.

What was my ultimate fishing adventure? Was it catching a 75-pound Alaskan chinook salmon on light tackle? Or maybe the 265-pound striped marlin in the Bay of Plenty, New Zealand on 30-pound test line? Perhaps one of the trophy Mexican black bass would qualify. Or the giant Snake River sturgeon I fought. I would certainly count my trophy sockeye salmon from Crescent Lake, Alaska as a candidate for this honor. Actually, though, I think the ultimate adventure of *any* fishing expedition is matching wits in a contest that demands all your abilities and talents.

That is why Jesus approached eight fishermen to be among His first disciples. These simple Galilean fishermen were rough and somewhat pedestrian in their thinking. Their Jewish roots, filled with passion and prejudice, often presented challenges to learning new ideas. These practical, hardworking men would soon give up their musty nets and smelly fish to catch the vision of Christ's ministry. Jesus said to them, "Come, follow me, and I will make you fishers of men" (Matthew 4:19).

Why does Jesus relate so well to fishermen and people of the out-of-doors? Fishermen are a unique breed and are rarely understood by others. More often than not, fishermen are considered a little odd or eccentric. Likewise, fishers of men do not lend themselves to a neat ecclesiastical job description.

Certainly there are many parallels between fishermen and disciples. Fishermen, for example, are inquisitive people of adventure and exploration. A disciple is never content with the routine and the mundane.

Fishermen are passionate. They spend countless hours preparing for, analyzing, evaluating, and pursuing their beloved sport. A disciple likewise attacks his mission with dedication and zeal.

Fishermen are people of skill and knowledge. They study the habits and habitats of fish while routinely practicing their casting skills. Similarly, fishers of men understand the sin-filled environment in which they live and work, while carefully devoting themselves to preparatory prayer and study.

Fishermen are eager to share their knowledge, experience, and skill with others. Disciples, too, are interested in sharing the joy of our Lord and Savior with others.

Fishermen catch fish. True disciples don't just fill a pew Sunday morning. They seek to "catch" others for Christ.

Now, as an outdoor writer I am well aware that many readers may not necessarily be familiar with all the jargon that goes along with this popular sport. After all, there are some 62 million fishermen in the United States, leaving another 200 million people wondering what we are all excited about.

A Little Lingo

Many nonfishermen think fishing is easy. They have never looked at a large fishing catalog with all the complicated equipment and paraphernalia. They have never worried about choosing between a "high modulus graphite composite with blank-thru-handle construction" or a "HSX Hi Strain graphite blank with aluminum oxide guides with Grade A specie cork grips."

Consider just a few of the terms a dedicated fisherman must know and understand before he sets out for the stream or lake: thermocline, topography, structure, breakline, ambush area, riprap, break point, buzz bait, double haul, roll cast, Texas rig, spinner bait, backtroll, high density, fast sink, Road Runner, suspended fish, Tournament Frog, pork rind, willow leaf, vibra shaft, Jiggle Tail, professional overspin, Slug-Go, Carolina rig, Yo-Bob, Jugbug, black lite, muddler minnow, wooly worm, crank bait, flippin', and pitchin'. The list goes on and on. The medical profession requires less technical jargon than the average fisherman.

It is not necessary for you to know all these terms. But there are a few important words I want to tell you about because they will come up throughout the rest of the book.

You will often come across the term *angler* in fishing circles. An angler is a sophisticated way of referring to a person who fishes with a rod, hook, and line as opposed to using dynamite or poison hemlock to capture trophies. (The Old English word *anga* meant "hook." An angler is hence one who uses a hook to fish.)

A *rod* is not a pole, unless you live below the Mason-Dixon line. Rods are used to fling or propel hooks, line, sinkers, bait, and lures in the general direction of a fish or tree—whichever comes first.

A *keeper* is the first fish you catch. If the fish's mouth is big enough to stretch over the barb (the sharp projection extending backward from the fishhook), then he is a keeper. There are several advantages to this definition. For example, what if the first fish you caught during the day was also the *only* fish you caught and you released it? Then you would have to go home *skunked*. Calling the first fish a keeper prevents the emotional trauma that results from going home empty-handed.

Further, as other fishermen inquire throughout the day how you are doing, you can reply in reference to the little fish about the size of your largest plug (or lure), "Just one keeper." The phrase, "Just one keeper," also suggests that you are a sportsman and have released all other fish.

If you are fortunate enough to fool another fish, you now have a small *mess*. If the second fish is bigger than the first fish, then you have a keeper and a badly hooked dink. You kept the dink (the small fish) because it was going to die anyway. This shows you care about the environment and pollution.

Using terms such as these will help establish you as a competent fisherman and one who can surely boast with the best of them.

As we consider how fishing relates to discipleship, it is clear that Jesus sought to relate to men who understood the challenges of life in a unique way—men who dealt with the mysteries of nature. He realized that many of the principles, methods, and techniques used in relating to people on a spiritual basis are similar to those used in fishing. By showing the disciples how to apply His teachings, they could then pursue the ultimate fishing challenge—*becoming fishers of men*.

The Ultimate Challenge

My heart's desire is that this book would be an encouragement for those who are not yet disciples, a guide and challenge to those who consider themselves followers, and a practical collection of biblical principles that a fisherman can use in catching fish *and* men. I trust this book will help you develop new skills and maturity through a careful study of practical discipleship.

Being a committed, effective Christian in many ways parallels the process of becoming a master fisherman. First, there must be a decision. Tell yourself, "I want to be the best fisherman I can be." Making the decision is often the biggest hurdle. It involves counting the cost—the time, the effort, and the study required. After deciding to become a good fisherman, the next step is to seek out the real pros.

You will want to carefully study the masters for information and techniques that will help you become a better angler. Observe their fishing abilities; become their disciple. Trust and give heed to their instructions and be guided by their encouragement.

Part of my training included analyzing numerous books, videotapes, and films on the subject. I had the privilege of fishing with my master-teachers—men such as Jimmy Houston, Al Lindner, Bobby Murray, Bill Norman, Jimmy Rogers, and other regional experts. As I further identified with their style, I became a disciple—a "learner" or "pupil."

During my competitive years, I sought to fish with the masters at every opportunity. In so doing I grew in my wisdom and understanding of fishing.

In the first century, an apprenticeship system was used to train spiritual leaders. Those in training attached themselves to a rabbi and literally lived with him for a period of time. Their goal was both to learn all their teacher knew and to imitate his way of life.

The disciples were called *Talmudim* during Jesus' ministry. In the first century it was common for groups of followers to attach themselves to traveling rabbis, becoming mobile *yeshivas* or schools. Because Jesus spoke with authority and performed miracles, many flocked to Him. The Greek word for disciple, *mathetes*, means "to learn." Therefore, a disciple is a "learner," "pupil," or "student."

As I researched the word "disciple," I found two elements

that apply. A disciple must have a certain *attitude* and resulting *actions* if he is to be a true disciple.

A fisherman teaches his trade to an apprentice one step at a time. Because there are so many variables in fishing, repetitive sessions are often needed to thoroughly acquaint an angler with all the possible alternatives. Likewise, a disciple will often learn best by experiencing a teaching through custom or habit.

The eminent Greek scholar Joseph H. Thayer suggested that a disciple is "a special kind of learner—one who learns by use and practice." [1] I am sure that James, the half brother of Jesus, must have realized this principle when he wrote, "Prove yourself doers of the word, and not merely hearers who delude themselves" (James 1:22 NASB).

A disciple is a *leader-in-training*. Disciples so identify with the master's attitudes and actions that they themselves become leaders. The process begins by receiving Christ as Lord and Savior. One then becomes a true learner. A disciple is perpetually learning, growing, and preparing to teach others as he himself matures.

Discipleship produces growth and evidence of maturity in wisdom and judgment. A disciple is a learner-in-process who in his lifestyle daily becomes more and more like Christ.

Jesus knew these men for several months before He called them to become disciples. In his book *Jesus Christ, Disciple Maker*, Bill Hull suggests,

> These men followed Jesus at His bidding because they had already been with Him. A chronological review of the disciples' exposure to Jesus reveals that during the initial four-month "Come and see" period, they received an intensive exposure to Jesus and to the nature of ministry. [2]

During this period, these men engaged in life-changing discussions with Jesus. They witnessed His miracles, listened to His teaching, and lived with Him. Jesus was a houseguest of the fisherman Peter and his family for at least two years during His three-and-a-half-year ministry.

Much like my study of our national pros, the disciples sat at Jesus' feet and listened to His every word. They studied His methods and adapted His teachings to their everyday life.

When on the shores of the Sea of Galilee, Jesus offered His challenge to these respected fishermen. He wanted them to *count the cost.*

"Come, follow me," Jesus said, "and I will make you fishers of men." In saying, "Come, follow me," Jesus was asking each fisherman to follow and believe in Him. In saying, "I will make you fishers of men," He was informing them, "I will now give you a ministry." A true disciple, then, will have a sincere belief *and* resulting action if he is going to be effective in reaching others for the kingdom.

Unlike a fisherman whose catch merely yields something to eat or something to brag about, Jesus wanted His disciples to "catch men" so that these men in turn could be released for service. And remember—unlike fishing for fish, it is never out of season to fish for souls.

The discipleship concept worked well in the first century and it still works today. The disciples didn't just learn from Jesus and stop there. They went out and *taught others* what they learned.

Despite the many similarities between fishing for trout or bass and fishing for men, there is a key difference as well. Jesus indicated to Peter, a seasoned angler of fish, that from now on he would be taking men alive" (see Luke 5).

Peter Marshall illuminated this passage when speaking at the University of Pittsburgh in 1946. He said, "Fishing for fish is pulling fish out of life into death. Fishing for men is pulling them out of death into life."

That, my friends, is what this book is all about! Tighten up your drags and sharpen your hooks because you are about to embark on what I term "the ultimate fishing challenge."

As with fishing, the disciple never wants to give up on

the challenge. Every fisherman has experienced the temptation and occasional success of making just one more cast into waters that look promising, hoping to land that last fish before the end of the day.

And so it is with being a disciple in the twenty-first century. As the time of our Lord's return draws near, we prepare to make "one more cast" to a waiting soul in the marketplace of *Promising Waters*. "Now is the day of salvation" (2 Corinthians 6:2).

While sharing a rich variety of fishing stories and adventures in this book, we will together explore the discipleship principles involved in following Jesus.

PROMISING WATERS

Chapter One

Commitment to the Task
"My Last Tournament"

In the late 1970s, my success on the western black bass tournament trail grew with each event. Fishing was becoming the passion of my life. I was now being asked to co-host fishing television programs, do demonstrations at major sports shows, and write for several major publications. In addition, a community college asked me to teach three classes a week on fishing.

All this on top of my accomplishments in public administration and my award-winning park and recreation programs placed me among the top administrators on the west coast. My MPA (Master of Public Administration degree) and other academic achievements qualified me to advance quickly in the organizations I served.

The climb to the top had not been easy. It required that I make some personal sacrifices along the way. My faith and my family had been put on the back burner so I could chase the "great American dream"—*success.*

I was fortunate when it came to family. God gave me a wonderful wife with enormous patience and love. Louise was the glue that kept our growing family together. Our gifted twin sons—Dan and Tom—required special attention and a great deal of Louise's time. The kids were a special blessing and, of course, I took most of the credit for that, too.

After a childhood of low self-esteem and hard knocks, I found it difficult to adjust to all the good things happening in my life without being prideful. I began to think I could do no wrong. But I was just kidding myself.

This brings to mind a fishing story that perfectly illustrates the overconfidence and arrogance I displayed during that time in my life. One of the nation's top fishing pros had become so successful that he was regularly invited to give talks about his techniques. To save time and prepare himself for the lectures, he hired a driver at minimum wage.

The pro was earning over $1,000 per lecture and was feeling pretty good about himself. After hearing about 50 seminars, the driver commented that he could probably give the same lecture and people would never know the difference.

The pro was fascinated with the driver's comment and decided to test the theory by trading places with him at the next stop. The chauffeur got all decked out with the pro's shirt and took the podium as the real pro stood in the back of the room observing. Sure enough the chauffeur did a great job and had the audience totally convinced that he was a professional.

Just as the chauffeur completed his last thought, however, a gentleman in the back asked him an extremely technical question about using electronic fish finders. To avoid giving himself away, and to maintain his prideful appearance, the chauffeur responded to the inquiry, "You know that really is an easy question; in fact, I believe my chauffeur [the real 'pro'] standing in the back of the room can even answer that."

Like the chauffeur, I had begun to think I had all the answers to everything. I had seen enough good parents and heard a few sermons on God's plan for the home. I thought I could fake all this to most onlookers.

By all *outward* appearances, I was a successful businessman, fisherman, college professor, outdoor writer, consultant, husband, and father. To top it all off, I received a new Ranger consignment bass boat that was the envy of every friend I had. Life was very good to me. But was it as fulfilling as I wanted it to be?

My wife did not think so. She arranged for us to attend James Dobson's parenting conference at Mount Hermon Christian Conference Center in the Santa Cruz mountains. I had no tournaments scheduled and no excuse for not attending. My only consolation was that my good friend and fishing buddy, Jerry, had also been roped in to this event by his wife, and we would drive to the camp together.

As we made our way to the conference center, Jerry and his wife Jeanie shared their plans to adopt a little girl from Chile. They asked me, "What does it take to be a good parent?" I said boastfully, "Just spend some quality time with the kids and they will do just fine."

My idea of being a successful parent was to beat the national average for quality time that dads spend each day with their children—*37.5 seconds*. I did that every night when I came home from my night meetings. I would go into the boys' room with a flashlight to see how much they had grown since my last visit. I prayed over them and tenderly kissed them good night.

Dr. Dobson was already preaching as we walked in on the first session. Within ten minutes, he informed us he would no longer be doing conference programs because it was taking too much time away from his family. He then explained that kids need both quality *and* quantity time from *both parents* if they are to be well adjusted and at a low risk for the type of teen problems we see every night on the evening news.

I immediately felt three sets of eyes peering at me as if I was some sort of trash fish—*and I was*. The reality is that I had been trying to be important instead of doing what was important according to God. I was totally out of balance, and my life was in chaos.

During that weekend conference, I got down on my

knees and asked God to help me reorder my private world. I came home and sorted out my "in-basket of life."

I weeded out the urgent tasks and duties from the important eternal concerns of life. My faith, my wife, my children, other family members, and friends who did not know Jesus Christ as their personal Savior quickly made their way to the top of my priority list.

That next year Louise's dad unexpectedly went to be with the Lord. He was the one who taught me how to bass fish. When he passed on, I had a tremendous sense of guilt. I recounted the many missed opportunities of asking him to accompany me on some of my fishing events.

His death opened my eyes to the temporary nature of this thing we call life. I looked around at all my "yuppie" friends who were so married to their work that they too were missing out on opportunities. I could now see more clearly the path I had previously chosen.

I reflected on people who had been my mentors and role models. I never heard of a dying man who said, "I wish I could have worked a little harder and made a little more money." I do, however, know of people with regrets about the little time they spent doing God's business and developing eternal relationships, especially with family members.

That winter I fished my last tournament and dedicated the victory to my father-in-law, Elmer Etter. I said good-bye to all my fishing buddies and suggested that we keep in touch. It was with some relief that I quit the competition scene because I was beginning to see the dark and prideful side of myself.

The next summer, our family attended a family conference at Mount Hermon featuring an aspiring young pastor, Chuck Swindoll. His open and authentic communication helped me see the wisdom of decisions I had made during the past eight months.

I had given up part-time teaching, consulting, and writing. No longer were there tournaments to fish. The pressure at work had been refocused. I now knew our boys in a different and exciting way, discovering many of their virtues and qualities that previously went unnoticed.

I began to know my children so well that I could tell how their day had gone just by watching their gait and posture as they walked to the car to be picked up from school. My love for my family grew tremendously.

Louise and I studied everything we could about balancing life's priorities and building strong families. My study of Scripture was consistent, as I took the same passion that previously drove me for personal gain and applied it to teaching others about the love of Jesus and the importance of strong families.

Life then threw me a punch. Three years after my "reorganization," I began to experience heart problems. It seemed as if my heart was stopping and on occasion my blood pressure would rise to the point that my head would ache. After seeing three separate heart doctors, it was determined that my problems were most likely stress-related.

After a visit to my internist, we agreed that the only thing left unchecked was a tinnitus (ringing noise) problem in my right ear. This problem is usually a benign condition. We suspected it had been caused by my involvement in sport shooting (another hobby). I had received a hearing test by an ear-nose-throat specialist just two years earlier with good results.

I was sent to a new specialist, however, and he decided to analyze this problem in more detail. After an initial x-ray study, the doctor discovered that I had a brain tumor. This news shook me to my very soul. The words I most feared to hear came from the mouth of that radiologist—*a tumor*.

As I was referred to yet another specialist, it became clear that this tumor was probably not cancerous but was a large growth called an acoustic neuroma. The problem was that this five-centimeter tumor was lodged into the brain stem at the point called the "message center." The heart and blood pressure are controlled from this part of the brain and no one was quite sure what would happen when the tumor was removed.

The weekend before surgery, I took my family to a

friend's home in the California delta to celebrate our 15-year wedding anniversary as well as an early birthday for our sons. It was a special time for all of us as we reflected on life. My fishing efforts produced a scrappy three-pound black bass that I stared at for some time before releasing. My boys could read my thoughts, "Will this be the last fish I ever catch?"

That next Tuesday afternoon, my father picked me up to take me to the hospital for an evening check-in. I delayed leaving home until my sons returned from school so I could get just one more hug and kiss from them and say my final good-byes.

Our tears flowed freely as we embraced. Their quivering 11-year-old bodies told me that the last three years of intimate time had not been enough. Our love had just started to blossom and their need for an encouraging, supportive dad would be greater in those fragile teenage years. The years when a boy chooses the pathway for life is when he is most vulnerable to the temptations of the world. This is a time when a boy needs a buddy and friend who can provide him with unconditional love.

As the car rolled out of the driveway, I looked back to see them huddled up with Louise. I wondered, *Have I given them enough of myself? Have I taught them the eternal truths of God's grace and mercy? Do they have what it takes to mature in their Christian commitment?*

Because of God's grace and miraculous power, my 9½-hour surgery was completely successful. No heart stopping, no vegetative state; only a loss of hearing and balance on my right side. I tell people I can no longer play the guitar, but I couldn't play it before anyway.

By allowing me to live, I knew God was not finished with me yet. After six weeks and much therapy, I could see clearly and walk again. I returned to life knowing that God was giving me the opportunity to become all He wanted me to be. *There would be no more wasted time.*

More than ever, I was committed to maintaining my family priorities while trying to provide guidance to other families who were in need of help. I had a special burden for the "workaholic dad" who by all appearances had torn out of his Bible the admonishments Timothy and Titus provided about balance and family.

With this revitalized outlook on life, Let's Go Fishing Ministries was formed. The goal of our ministry is to help traditional and single-parent families discover Jesus Christ and the value of a "Christian leisure ethic." Let's Go Fishing Ministries later spawned a national organization called The Fellowship Of Christian Anglers Society (FOCAS) which places traditional family values at the forefront of its agenda. Simply put—its purpose is to train disciples and strengthen families.

Most of all, my experience in the hospital gave me a new appreciation for those who do not yet know Jesus Christ as their personal Savior. When you are at death's doorstep, the issue of where you want to spend eternity is of utmost concern. You give deep and reflective thought to who will be joining you and to those close friends and relatives who have not yet accepted God's saving grace.

How is it with you? *Have you given thought to who will be joining you in eternity?*

As you read this book, with its many stories about fishing and following Jesus, may God motivate you to participate in the ultimate fishing adventure! Indeed, may God motivate you to become a fisher of men.

Personal Growth

- How does Jesus define "success"?

- Are you a Christian? You cannot be one of Jesus' disciples until you have entered into a personal relationship with Him. (Read Romans 3:23; 5:1-8; 10:9; Ephesians 2:8-9; Isaiah 59:2; and John 1:12.)

Priorities
"Lost in the Fog"

It was a cold December morning in the San Francisco Bay area. The weather forecast indicated there was a chance of showers with heavy fog in the inland areas. I rolled out of bed before daybreak and had a light breakfast, said good-bye to my sleeping family, and headed my rig down the road to pick up my fishing buddy, Rick.

It was Rick's first day out since his tragic industrial accident and he was not sure if he was up to boating and fishing. I saw his apprehension as I looked into his eyes.

Rick was a quiet sort of guy, a member of our Castro Valley Bass Classics for about two years. He seemed unusually quiet as we loaded his gear into my Suburban. The uneasiness within his spirit was apparent.

Rick had been a gifted climber who worked the steel beams on high-rise structures. His job involved climbing vertical columns of steel without safety equipment or machinery to assist him.

Several months before our trip, Rick had scaled a column to the 30-foot level, walked out on a horizontal beam to direct a crane operator, and hit an icy area. He fell 30 feet, landing on a pile of rubble. The impact shattered his lower back. His initial prognosis had not been good.

Rick and I were close for the several weeks after his accident. Miraculously, he regained fairly good use of his legs. Now it was time to talk about retraining and a change of vocation. During his recovery, he expressed concern that he might never fish or even walk again.

We headed east toward the Sacramento River delta, not paying much attention to road conditions. It's typically foggy over the pass at this time of year, although it's not often dense.

As we arrived at the marina, I commented to Rick that it was going to be a challenge to see many birds diving for bait fish with the heavy fog conditions. I noticed that the marina parking lot was empty. *That should have told me something.*

Climbing aboard, we launched the boat into the heavy mist. I could tell Rick was feeling very uneasy about motoring off into this strange environment. But I reassured him that all was fine. After all, he was with one of the top fishermen in California and a man who knew the delta well.

It was important to motor along at idling speed since we could not see beyond the front of the boat. We used the dark shadows of the old sunken barges on the starboard side as a reference point. If we just followed this line of sunken barges, we would soon come to my favorite slough.

We were out for about 15 minutes when we came to the last barge. All we had to do was cross this slough and waiting for us on the rocky far bank would be five-pound black bass and several of their striped bass cousins. I had caught and released them just a few days earlier.

The biting cold and the endless fog seemed to worsen as we moved across the slough. We needed to correct our steering to the right if we were going to run a correct course. My boat tended to pull to the left when motoring at low speeds.

We had been totally quiet for about five minutes. Finally, Rick broke the silence and asked, "When will we get there?"

He was obviously getting anxious. I tried to reassure

him. Deep down, though, I knew something was wrong. I had miscalculated the mark. Perhaps I had overcorrected the steering. I guess I was too proud to stop and admit my confusion. After ten minutes of fruitless efforts, however, I had thoroughly convinced both of us that I had no idea where we were.

The river current was running quickly, and I visualized my new Ranger bass boat drifting under the Golden Gate Bridge and out to sea without anyone noticing. What a ridiculous situation we found ourselves in.

I turned off the engine and stared into the fog. Why on earth had I left the marina, let alone my nice warm bed? Rick's stress level was building with every passing moment. The idea of going fishing had been to get his mind off such things as death, tension, and himself—*and* to redirect his negative thinking. Our present situation was not helping matters.

We drifted for what seemed like hours, although it was only 15 to 20 minutes. If that weren't bad enough, a noise began to emerge from the fog. Terror began to grip my heart as I realized it was the sound of the propeller wash of a very large ship. Russian ships regularly enter San Francisco Bay and move up the Sacramento River to the San Joaquin River in Stockton, where they load their empty hulls with grain from several riverside locations.

As this ship steamed up the river with its radar on, I knew they were hoping not to hit any obstructions. Why the skipper hadn't picked a clear day to move upriver puzzled me. We were sitting somewhere near this approaching ship in a relatively small fiberglass boat that seldom shows up on radar. *Was it headed in our direction? Should we move? What direction?* We decided to stay where we were and pray.

The ship passed on our port side, probably 150 feet away. We heard every beat of the prop blades hitting the water. It was close enough that the wake nearly capsized my boat. It was a close call we would remember for life.

As I thought about this brush with near-tragedy, I was

reminded of how often Jesus' disciples became sidetracked, frightened, and even lost. Their priorities were regularly tested.

Even Jesus challenged the disciples' personal growth and development as spiritual leaders when He asked them, "Why are you timid, you men of little faith" (Matthew 8:26 NASB). Wasn't He really asking them, "Why don't you have your spiritual priorities in better order?" Jesus knew they needed to mature in their faith, yet He remained sensitive to their frustrations and confusion. To help them better define their priorities, He offered them a simple but profound message—the Sermon on the Mount—that we can read about in Matthew 5–7.

On a hill (or mount) above Tabgha, a town located on the western shores of the unpredictable Sea of Galilee, Jesus taught His disciples about the importance of not being lost in the influence of the world's value system. He reminded them that meekness, gentleness, humility, mercy, purity, forgiveness, and integrity are important characteristics of a disciple (Matthew 5:1-10).

Jesus also emphasized that God knew their every need, and if they would first seek God's kingdom, He would bless them with all that they needed (Matthew 6:33). He taught them the basics of setting priorities and maintaining trust that would change their lives forever.

My mind then shifted back to the present. As we continued to sit in the boat on that cold, damp day, I remembered God's promises. I called on Him to protect us and guide us out of this dilemma.

Suddenly it occurred to me that there was a compass and a map somewhere in the boat's glove box. Scrambling to my feet, I dug around for these important navigational tools. Grabbing them, I questioned what good they would be without some idea of where we were. Staring at them, I wondered what to do next.

An insistent foghorn off our port bow finally penetrated my consciousness. And there was a train moving along the tracks off the stern. The sounds were at some distance, but they were recognizable. *We could read our position from them.*

With the compass and map, we calculated that the boat should be turned 180 degrees to find the marina. It was difficult to trust these aids because my instincts told me otherwise. But I fixed my gaze on the tools at hand and moved in the new direction by total faith.

Would you believe it? We went about 200 yards and the dark outline of the marina began to appear. "We're home Rick. Do you still want to go fishing?" I asked.

"Jim, I think we've had enough excitement for one day. Let's go get some breakfast!" was his welcome reply.

Strange as this incident was, I have heard other boaters share similar experiences. One of the most humorous involved two Kiwi (New Zealand) fishermen, Andy and Mark. These two lads pushed off from shore in heavy fog and headed to their favorite fishing hole located just off the Bay of Plenty Coast of the North Island.

They continued to motor along in the dense fog until Andy was convinced they were exactly where they should be. The day before, he had experienced some great action in that area. In reality, Andy wasn't sure where they were, but he convinced his buddy Mark they should cast into the fog toward what he thought was a submerged reef area.

Shortly after their baits landed, they began to feel several bites. They continued to set the hooks with every bite, but would only reel in a clean hook. After going through a bucket of bait, the fog finally lifted. *Were they ever embarrassed!* Apparently, their direction was off, and they had been casting onto a sandy shoreline. A flock of seagulls was enjoying every bit of food these two anglers were willing to provide.

I believe we can learn an important lesson from these stories. We need to better understand our limitations. Without a clear understanding of who we are and how God can direct and guide our lives, we will be "lost in the fog."

The "fog of life" is anything that clutters our focus on God's plan for our lives. For many of us, the "fog" is the pursuit of materialism. To some, it is being so focused on one's job that relationships suffer. To others, the abuse of authority and power is a "fog" that has caused them to lose their way in life. Still others deal with a midlife crisis by pursuing an extramarital affair that creates an illusion of happiness.

As we trust in the Lord to guide us, our lives will transcend those issues that would otherwise entrap and distract us from following the right course. By having Christ-centered priorities in order, we can steady our ways and become true disciples.

King Solomon once advised, "Let your eyes look straight ahead, fix your gaze directly before you. Make level paths for your feet and take only ways that are firm. Do not swerve to the right or the left; keep your foot from evil" (Proverbs 4:25-27).

Navigational Tools for Successful Living

What keeps us on track? What resources can we use when we are "lost in the fog of life"?

God has filled our personal "boats" with all kinds of helpful tools to assist with the challenges of life. He has given us a whole range of helps so we can avoid being "lost in the fog."

The Bible—"A Lamp to My Feet"

First, there is the Bible, which is like a map that guides and directs our lives. It helps us to understand *where we have been*, *where we are*, and *where we are going*. It is a light that illuminates our course through uncharted waters and stormy seas. The psalmist said, "Your word is a lamp to my feet and a light for my path" (Psalm 119:105).

The Bible also functions as an internal guidance system. As the psalmist put it, "I have hidden your word in my heart that I might not sin against you" (Psalm 119:11).

James, the half brother of Jesus, describes how we should use this helpful resource: "Do not merely listen to the word, and so deceive yourselves. Do what it says" (James 1:22). *Catch that?* The Bible can and should be our map—our resource manual to chart the proper course for life. It does us very little good, however, *unless we follow it*.

The Holy Spirit—Our Inner Compass

The Holy Spirit provides an inner compass to guide our conscience (Romans 9:1). With the ever-changing moral codes of our society, it is helpful to know that the Holy Spirit is consistent from age to age. He will not fail us.

When the Holy Spirit fills us, we are enabled to face the challenges before us (Ephesians 5:18). If we listen carefully to the still quiet voice of the Holy Spirit, He will point us in the right direction (1 Corinthians 2:12). We might say that we are useless "flashlights" until the "batteries" of the Holy Spirit energize us for service and worship (see Galatians 5:22).

Prayer—Communicating with God

Prayer is a special communication system with God Almighty. Through prayer we can go to God and share our dreams, concerns, fears, ambitions, requests, and praise (Philippians 4:6). As a foghorn helps direct a lost fisherman back to port, so an active prayer life gives guidance and vision to help us through the fog of life.

So important was prayer to Christ that He often withdrew from the crowds for the sole purpose of praying (Luke 5:16). Prayer was so important to His disciples' personal growth that He gave them a model prayer as a guide (Matthew 6:5-15).

In his book *How to Pray*, E. Stanley Jones tells us that "prayer is not only the refuge of the weak; it is the reinforcement of the strong."[1] Prayer isn't just for bluegill fishermen or lost boaters—*it's for you and me*. Remember, the greatest fisherman who ever lived—Jesus Christ—saturated His life with prayer (Mark 1:35; 6:46).

Jones goes on to suggest that "prayer is not bending God to my will, but it is a bringing of my will into conformity with God's will, so that His will may work in and through me."[2] You might look at it this way: When you are in a small boat and you throw out a boat hook to catch hold of the shore, do you pull the shore to yourself, or do you pull yourself to the shore? "Prayer is not bending the universe to your will, making God a cosmic bellhop for your purposes, but prayer is cooperating with the purposes of God to do things you never dreamed you could do."[3]

Christian Fellowship—Mutual Support

Christian fellowship is another "navigational tool" the Lord has given to us for successful living. My fellowship with Rick enabled both of us to face our fears with courage and support. Faithful and encouraging friends can strengthen us to face those uncharted waters. And fellow believers hold us accountable so we can grow and stay on course.

Thinking back to that day with Rick, it was only by fixing our gaze upon our resources that we were able to take a bad boating decision and find a positive outcome. So too, using the "navigational tools" and resources Christ has given us helps us to keep our lives on track. Keeping our personal priorities in order—with Christ Himself being the *top* priority—prevents us from sinking into the circumstances of daily living.

Christ will keep you from getting "lost in the fog."

Personal Growth

- Are you "lost in the fog of life?" What adjustments do you need to make in your priorities?

- What is your "map" for living?

- Scripture says God's Word is a lamp to our feet and a light for our path (Psalm 119:105). Can you establish a routine to absorb God's guidance daily?

- What are some lessons we can learn about prayer from the teachings of Christ in Matthew 6:5-15?

Preparation and Presentation
"The Right Cast"

O ne of my favorite fishing stories comes from my good friend, Jimmy Houston. Jimmy is one of the greatest anglers of all time. His winsome ways and jovial spirit have endeared him to the hearts of fishermen everywhere.

Perhaps Jimmy's greatest asset is his love of the Lord with an unbridled passion. He continually applies God's Word to daily living. He is truly a disciple of the Lord Jesus.

No one works harder at preparing for a tournament and presenting a lure correctly than Jimmy. He is a 14-time Bass Classic qualifier and has won every major casting contest he has entered. His underhand casting technique enables him to present rapid casts to difficult areas with very little effort.

We have fished in the same boat many times. Jimmy usually operates in tight quarters in the midst of brush and trees. His presentations are extremely accurate and cover every predictable spot.

Needless to say, it is intimidating to compete against this champ. He is like a human vacuum cleaner, sucking up every fish within reach.

Years ago Jimmy was at a Bassmaster tournament and drew a local "good ol' boy" named Elton Jones as his partner. It was a bright calm day as the sun came up behind the docks. Elton, dressed in his bib overalls and plaid shirt, was standing at the appointed place with a big smile, a very large picnic basket, a single rod, and a little brown bag of fishing tackle.

Jimmy came by the dock and said, "Hop in, Elton. Where is your tackle?"

Elton replied, "I've got all I need, Jimmy. I'll be just fine."

As Jimmy took off from the docks, he couldn't help but think, "I surely won't have to worry about competition from Elton. This is going to be a snap."

Jimmy asked Elton if he wanted the first part of the day or the last half. It is customary for tournament fishermen to choose which part of the day they will take the front of the boat. The person up front gets to determine what part of the lake they want to fish.

Elton replied that he only wanted the front of the boat for one hour—from one to two o'clock.

After racing to the first spot, Jimmy began to make his rapid casts, frantically thrashing the water with his spinner bait. About 20 minutes passed when Jimmy realized Elton had yet to make a cast. Jimmy turned around to make sure Elton was still in the boat and discovered him sitting on the pro-throne seat with a large cup of coffee, eating a chocolate donut.

Elton smiled at Jimmy and said, "Want a cup of coffee or a donut?"

Jimmy politely refused, turned around, and just kept fishing, knowing that every cast was a new opportunity to introduce a fish to his spinner bait.

After an hour or so, Jimmy felt guilty that he had the water to himself and thought he ought to tell Elton it was okay for him to fish when he was on Jimmy's spot.

Elton said, "I am enjoying watching you work so hard, Jimmy."

After another hour, Jimmy hooked a fish and yelled to Elton to "get the net." Elton quickly obliged. He jumped off his chair and grabbed the net, scooping in a keeper fish. About a half hour later, Jimmy caught another one. Again, Elton scooped in the fish.

Elton still had not made a cast, or even set up his rod. Jimmy was beginning to wonder if Elton was one of Roland Martin's spies, taking notes on all Jimmy was doing. (Roland Martin, a winner of many bass tournaments, hosts a national TV show on fishing.)

Not much later Jimmy heard Elton moving around in the back of the boat. When Jimmy looked at Elton this time, he could not believe his eyes. Elton had taken the back seat off the deck and laid it on the floor between the two fishermen. He was spreading a large red and white checked tablecloth on the deck and was proceeding to unpack his picnic basket. He laid out a three-course, fried chicken lunch.

Elton asked, "Jimmy, how about taking a break and having some lunch?"

Jimmy thought, "I can't believe this guy. Doesn't he know that this is a major tournament and that every second counts?"

At one o'clock, Elton picked up his lunch and began to rig his rod. Jimmy noticed a handful of mini-jigs (small lures) and some leader material (high quality fishing line) that Elton was assembling. Jimmy looked at Elton and said "Well, it's your turn. Where do you want to go?"

Elton said, "I would like you to pull away from this shoreline you've been beatin' on all morning and go out to the middle of the lake, about 300 yards from the little island." Jimmy reluctantly followed his orders and motored over to this quiet, nondescript area.

Looking around with some consternation, Jimmy asked, "Are you sure you want to be out here?"

Elton indicated it was the right spot, and said, "keep an eye out for bait fish."

Elton stood up, grabbed his rod, and began to survey the

water like a hawk looking for prey. Jimmy sat there with his spinner bait dangling, wondering how he was going to fish this open water.

Just about that time a large school of shad started dancing on the surface in an area about three times the size of the boat. Before Jimmy could evaluate the situation, Elton's cast was on the way with mini-jigs flying left and right.

As the jigs began to sink, Elton reached back and set the hook, yelling out, "One!" A few seconds later, he set the hook again, yelling out, "Two!" The routine was repeated until Jimmy heard, "Five!"

With his rod bent double, Elton shouted to Jimmy, "Son, get the net." With a proud look and his rod flexed to the maximum, old Elton slowly reeled in his limit of keeper fish while Jimmy tried to scoop them up.

Five fish were brought aboard just as the bait fish scattered and submerged for another day. Jimmy grabbed his rod, changed lures, and frantically peppered the water with casts as Elton was unhooking his trophies. Elton reminded him that it was all in the preparation and the presentation. For Jimmy, there were many valuable lessons learned that day about having the *right lure*, at the *right time*, in the *right place*.

It is not only thoughtful fishermen who realize the importance of preparation and presentation. Thoughtful disciples realize this as well.

Many Christians take their Bibles and beat the waters of life without a specific plan and purpose. If they are fortunate enough to catch someone's interest with the gospel, it is more of an accident than a well thought-out effort. They are not selective or wise in thinking about discipling opportunities prior to sharing Scripture verses. They have not equipped themselves with the right attitude and approach to successfully present their testimony and the Word of God.

As believers, we have a responsibility to prepare ourselves for ministry. We are instructed, "Therefore, prepare your minds for action; be self-controlled; set your hope fully on the grace to be given you when Jesus Christ is revealed" (1 Peter 1:13).

We must also rely on the Holy Spirit. The Holy Spirit can prepare the person we hope to disciple by convicting and enlightening his or her heart (John 16:8-11). When this has been done, the person becomes open to receiving truth and encouragement.

Sometimes in our zeal to disciple others, we try to assume the responsibility of the Holy Spirit. This often leads to frustration and confusion. Remember, no individual has ever single-handedly brought another person into the kingdom. *The Holy Spirit must be the prompter.*

A Four-Step Checklist from Psalm 23

As we review Christ's life and teachings, we see a clear pattern that precedes His major presentations to the multitudes. He was always balanced, rested, focused, and mindful of God's power.

We see similar qualities reflected in the opening verses of Psalm 23. In fact, these verses lay out a four-step checklist that can help disciples become more effective in preparation and presentation regarding ministry opportunities.

Step One: Remember that Jesus Is Lord

The psalmist said, "The Lord is my Shepherd, I shall not be in want" (Psalm 23:1).

Disciples of Christ need to recognize and acknowledge that Jesus is Lord. If we are to be effective in our discipling, He must be preeminent in our thinking and actions. Because He is the sovereign Lord, He is truly a worthy shepherd.

There are many comforting verses that speak of the Lord's sovereignty. The psalmist said, "I will come and proclaim your mighty acts, O Sovereign Lord; I will proclaim your righteousness, yours alone" (Psalm 71:16). We are reminded by the psalmist that "the Lord has established His throne in the heavens; and His sovereignty rules over all" (Psalm 103:19 NASB). *Is Jesus Lord of your life?*

Step Two: Remember the Importance of Rest

The psalmist said of Christ our Shepherd, "He makes me lie down in green pastures" (Psalm 23:2a).

Christ often withdrew from the multitudes to physically rest and prepare His heart in quiet meditation before presenting His major messages (Matthew 14:13; Luke 4:42; Mark 6:31). Most often He was near the majestic Sea of Galilee where He could ponder God's infinite creation and revive His weary body with sleep and relaxation. Rest was a high priority for Him.

Rest should be a high priority for us as well. Indeed, physical rest is crucial to reduce stress and balance out our body chemistry. Without rest we deteriorate. That is why Christ's ministry of enabling us to "lie down in green pastures" is so vitally important. *Good disciples are rested disciples.*

Step Three: Remember that Spiritual Refreshment Is Vital

The psalmist said of Christ our Shepherd, "He leads me beside quiet waters" (Psalm 23:2b).

In our zeal as modern-day disciples, we often try to measure the effectiveness of our work (ministry) according to the volume of activity generated by our programs. God's design for work is that it would not be burdensome or detract from those quiet moments that can quench the thirst of our spirit (Matthew 11:28).

In properly preparing to minister (or fish), many of us forget to seek out the quiet waters of life where inspiration and refreshment abound. In our illustration above, Elton was always relaxed and refreshed. He sought out the quiet waters in the middle of the lake. He was away from the distraction of the shoreline. And in his refreshed state he was an incredibly competent fisherman. Elton was one who discovered the outpouring of blessing that can occur in those undisturbed moments of time.

Many of us are in the fast lane of life and would like to pull over at the next rest stop where we can obtain needed refreshment. How foolish it is to ignore the built-in pressure gauge God has given us that helps us limit our activities. Some who refuse to "pull over" will find their physical or emotional engines blowing up. They will be forced to the side of the road.

We need to take spiritual refreshment seriously. If we don't, we pay the consequences.

Step Four: Remember that God Guides and Directs Us

When Christ is at the center of our lives, our desire is to order our priorities so that we follow *His* prescription for wellness. It is then that our spirit is sensitive to His guidance and direction.

The psalmist tells us that Christ our Shepherd will guide us "in paths of righteousness" (Psalm 23:3b). He will lead us. He will direct us. And as we follow His lead, our lives become balanced and unstressed, focused in on God's plan for our lives.

A Disciple Is Always Prepared

Followers of Christ prepare for opportunities to share the good news of the gospel with others. We are admonished, "Always be prepared to give an answer to everyone who asks you to give the reason for the hope that you have" (1 Peter 3:15).

Presentation is critical to the ultimate results of both fishing *and* evangelism. The fisherman, for example, must continually practice presenting the lure correctly. Only then does he become a skilled fisherman. In like manner, the disciple must continually practice presenting the gospel message. The more he does so, the more effective he becomes as a fisher of men.

Remember, too, that different conditions often require the fisherman to use different baits. Similarly, when a disciple encounters a person who has a particular sensitivity or a need in a certain area, he can share the most appropriate message for that situation—a message of truth balanced with understanding and love.

We must also beware that there are many imitation lures that do not work nearly as effectively as the original high-quality product. Let us remember that vain philosophy and modern-day psychology do not produce the same effect as applying God's Word.

Finally, it is appropriate that we prepare ourselves with prayer so that we have the proper wisdom, timing, and knowledge on each of our "casts." We must sharpen our "hooks" of testimony so that, combined with sharing the gospel, they "lure in" and "catch" the inquiring hearts and minds of lost "fish."

Personal Growth

- What are some urgent-agenda items that are keeping you from experiencing a biblically balanced life?

- Are you seeking out the quiet places in life for those teachable moments with the Master?

- How did Jesus prepare for service? (Matthew 14:13; Luke 4:42; Mark 6:31)

- What lessons can you learn from the prayer life of Jesus? (Matthew 14:23, Mark 1:35, Luke 6:12)

Chapter Four

Concentration
"The Key to Fishing Success"

Denny Bauer is one of the most successful national bass tournament fishermen on the circuit. His award-winning strategies include such basics as concentrating on details and remaining totally focused on the events of the day.

Several years ago, Denny participated in a Bassmaster tournament in Louisiana. This was a particularly critical contest because of its impact on the year-end standings. Because of the importance of the event, Denny's level of concentration was even more intensely focused than usual.

As was the custom, each contestant was paired with another fisherman by computer matching. Denny arrived early the morning of the tournament to meet his partner, a local fisherman named Bubba.

Bubba was over six feet tall and weighed 280 pounds. He was dressed in a jumbo yellow rain suit, carried a handful of mismatched rods, and a bag full of lures.

Denny noticed that several of Bubba's spinning rods had bait-casting reels attached. Any serious fisherman knows you need a bait-casting rod with a good trigger grip to match those reels. This guy was obviously not a real fisherman and could be a hindrance to Denny's objectives.

Bubba was none too happy about getting up early to fish in the rain and growled that this "better be worth it!" The rain kicked up just as Denny took off at 65 miles per hour across the lake. Unfortunately, Bubba's seat did not have a console and windshield in front of him so he caught the full brunt of the wind and rain. After the long ride, Bubba glared at Denny with threatening looks. This intimidation shattered Denny's concentration.

Despite the weather, Denny's fish were on the bite. But ol' Bubba had missed several fish and was beginning to give Denny a hard time. Denny suggested that Bubba strike a little harder next time—he was not getting good hook penetration through the worm.

It was Bubba's turn for the next good spot. As he flipped his worm on the "brush pile" (the "ambush area" where the fish were suspected of "hiding out"), a spunky two-pounder decided to take Bubba for a walk. As the fish hit the worm, Bubba pulled back as hard as he could only to see his favorite rod slip out of his wet hands into the brush pile.

After some loud pronouncements, Bubba directed Denny to the spot where his rod disappeared. He began to reach out, balancing himself on the gunnel. As Bubba fell out of the boat, he tried to give Denny a short course in "break dancing" on water! According to Denny, "Bubba looked like a one-ton canary trying to take a bath."

Upon retrieving the rod and fish, Denny helped wrestle Bubba back into the boat. Though Denny was not finished fishing, Bubba suggested they *were both* through for the day. Denny's concentration and focus had been totally disrupted. As a result, he lost his effectiveness for the rest of the day.

The Disciples Learn a Faith Lesson

The story above reminds me of another fisherman who tried to walk on water almost 2,000 years ago. While the incident was very different, it taught the disciples the importance of focus and concentration.

Shortly after the miraculous feeding of 5,000 people, the disciples left in their boat and found themselves in the midst of a storm. The disciples had left according to Jesus' instructions. We read in Matthew 14:22-23:

> Immediately Jesus made the disciples get into the boat and go on ahead of him to the other side, while he dismissed the crowd. After he had dismissed them, he went up on a mountainside by himself to pray. When evening came, he was there alone.

Jesus wanted to be alone to communicate with the Father and to rest from His demanding ministry. Of course, God does not need to rest. But Jesus, who in the Incarnation was both God *and* man, needed to reenergize His body, mind, and spirit. He reclined on that gentle slope overlooking Tabgha Harbor on the northwest shore of the Sea of Galilee.

The fishermen-disciples had already begun their evening work. The Sea of Galilee—also known as Lake Gennesaret, Lake Kinnereth, or the Sea of Tiberias (named after the king)—was a familiar location for the disciples. They knew that the best fishing with trammel nets (gill nets) came in the evening hours when the small bait fish came to the surface along the shoreline, bringing the bigger "game fish" with them.

These young men were still considering the call Christ had made on their lives a few months earlier: "Come, follow me, and I will make you fishers of men" (Matthew 4:19). They were still sorting through what it meant to be a disciple. Their faith was young and, like most accomplished fishermen, they were depending upon their own abilities and skills.

We read in Matthew 14:24 that the disciples' boat was "a considerable distance from land, buffeted by the waves because the wind was against it." This took place "during the fourth watch of the night."

The disciples were having a tough time. The wind and

waves had driven them many yards from shore and the chill of the early morning hours was setting in. The "fourth watch" was from three to six o'clock in the morning when exhaustion hangs heavy and it seems it will never be daylight again. The imagination wanders and fear seems to heighten. The dampness clings and bites.

There were no comforting shoreline beacons in sight—and no lighted compasses aboard this old wooden boat. These tired fishermen were scared and disappointed. *Who's idea was this? Why didn't we stick with Jesus?* Their desperation may have drawn them into childish accusations.

At the point of their greatest concern, though, they saw Jesus. But they did not expect to encounter Jesus in this way. Scripture explains:

> Jesus went out to them, walking on the lake. When the disciples saw Him walking on the lake, they were terrified. "It's a ghost," they said, and cried out in fear. But Jesus immediately said to them: "Take courage! It is I. Don't be afraid." (Matthew 14:25-27)

In the original Greek, the word for *ghost* is literally "fantasm" or "fantom." The disciples thought they were seeing a ghost or a phantom spirit. But Jesus calmed the situation by announcing that it was He.

Peter was so impressed with this miracle that his immediate response was, "Lord, if it's you, tell me to come to you on the water" (Matthew 14:28). Peter is a lot like many of us—*impulsively direct!* Most fishermen are short on patience and quick to take action without thoroughly considering all the factors involved. Peter wanted to step out in faith—he wanted to be with Jesus.

Jesus said, "Come" (Matthew 14:29). Peter fixed his gaze upon the Lord and stepped onto the water. He did not walk around the boat or head off to a better fishing hole; *he walked on water and he walked straight toward Jesus.*

What happened to Peter next is the same thing that happens to all of us when we take our gaze off the Master—*we sink*. "But when [Peter] saw the wind, he was afraid and, beginning to sink, cried out, 'Lord, save me!' " (Matthew 14:30).

Peter broke contact with Jesus the moment his gaze became fixated on the wind. And how quickly he called out for help!

Isn't it great that we have a merciful God? "Immediately Jesus reached out his hand and caught him. 'You of little faith,' he said, 'why did you doubt?' " (Matthew 14:31). In His love and faithfulness, Jesus was there for Peter, just as He is always there for us (Psalm 57:3).

Jesus saved Peter and then calmed the waters of the sea. "When they climbed into the boat, the wind died down. Then those who were in the boat worshiped him, saying, 'Truly you are the Son of God' " (Matthew 14:32-33). Peter and the others realized that a mere man could not have done what they had just witnessed.

Life's Challenges: Opportunities to Trust God

Many of our daily tasks involve risk. Being a fisherman 2,000 years ago was no easy task. The unfriendly elements and poor equipment posed challenges. Most of the fishing was done in the dark of the evening hours when the sea was most dangerous. Today, our equipment is better. But sometimes our judgment is lacking, and we still have to fight those unfriendly elements.

In life we find continual challenges in our work environment, recreational activities, and family life. Our recession-riddled world continues to create stress on our ability to order our private world and balance life's priorities. Many families are working through the backwash of brokenness and bitterness, trying to piece things together.

All of us need to consider the challenges of life as opportunities to trust God. We need to look for ways to expand our horizon. Like Peter, we need to dare to step out in faith—

even taking *a risk* based on our faith. We may sometimes find ourselves battering the wind-currents of life. But there is always hope, no matter what we encounter. *God is with us*.

Do you need to take a risk in developing a new friendship? Perhaps your risk is changing careers so you can enjoy more time with your family. Or maybe your risk involves trusting someone who has let you down.

Helen Keller said this about risk: "Security is mostly a superstition. It does not exist in nature...Life is either a daring adventure or nothing." [1]

Risk requires that we recognize our inability to "go it alone"—*we need to trust the Lord*. We need the support of our Lord who can reach out and save us from the circumstances of life. Jesus says, "Take courage! It is I." *Are we really listening?* God wants us to trust Him—to take courage.

Perhaps the author of the wonderful poem, "Footprints," said it best. Listen to his words:

> "One night a man had a dream. He dreamed he was walking along the beach with the Lord. Across the sky flashed scenes of his life. For each scene he noticed two sets of footprints. One belonged to him and one to the Lord.
>
> When the last scene had flashed before him, he looked back at the footprints and noticed that many times along the path there was only one set of footprints in the sand. He also noticed that this happened during the lowest and saddest times of his life.
>
> This really bothered him and he questioned the Lord. "Lord, you said that once I decided to follow you, you would never leave me, and that you would walk all the way with me. But I noticed that during the troublesome times of my life there was only one set of footprints. I don't understand why you deserted me."
>
> The Lord replied, "My precious, precious child, I love you and I would never leave you. During your

times of trial and suffering, when you see only one set of footprints, it was then that I carried you."[2]

Peter certainly found this to be true. When Peter "sank" in the circumstances of life, the Lord carried him. He does the same with each of us.

Fixing Our Gaze Upon Jesus

Peter had fixed his gaze upon Jesus. We might define "gaze" as a look that penetrates to the heart—*a concentrated focus*. Peter concentrated his focus on the Lord Jesus. You and I need to do the same.

When we are truly focused upon our Lord with our prayer life, our worship, and our actions, *He Himself* handles our problems and conquers our fears. He makes us strong and able to walk boldly and with confidence (Proverbs 3:26).

How often we fail in maintaining our focus on Christ. The distractions and encumbrances of life surround us and we feel smothered. We need the fresh spirit of Jesus that resuscitates us to life—*eternal* life. Psalm 27:4 states, "One thing I ask of the Lord, this is what I seek: that I may dwell in the house of the Lord all the days of my life, *to gaze upon the beauty of the Lord and to seek him in his temple*" (emphasis added).

David C. Needham, in his marvelous book *Close to His Majesty*, speaks of the great intimacy that results when we focus our gaze upon God:

> It is so easy to forget that God saved us above all else for love, for intimacy in relationship, for response. To fail to have time for this is to fail at living. Certainly His intentions are that everything else—service, witnessing, practical holiness—be a byproduct of our love for Him. And nurturing love takes time. Where did we ever get the idea that it simply "happens?" It doesn't.[3]

In Proverbs 4:24-25 we find the counsel of the great King Solomon. Despite his wealth, wisdom, and fame, he reminds us of the most important thing—*keeping focused on God*: "Put away perversity from your mouth; keep corrupt talk far from your lips. Let your eyes look straight ahead, fix your gaze directly before you."

When distractions well up, seeking to draw our attention away from Christ, *that* is the most important time to keep our gaze—*our concentration*—focused solely upon Him. The author of Hebrews put it this way:

> Therefore, since we are surrounded by such a great cloud of witnesses, let us throw off everything that hinders and the sin that so easily entangles, and let us run with perseverance the race marked out for us. Let us fix our eyes on Jesus, the author and perfecter of our faith, who for the joy set before him endured the cross, scorning its shame, and sat down at the right hand of the throne of God. (Hebrews 12:1-2)

To be effective disciples, then, you and I must fix our eyes upon Jesus. As we keep our gaze focused on Him, all else in our lives will be seen in proper perspective. No problem seems too big—*for He is always with us.*

Personal Growth

- Is your gaze focused more on your problems or on the Lord? Do you need to adjust your focus?

- What challenges are you facing that are great opportunities to trust the Lord?

Chapter Five

Faith
"A Vision for Fishing"

In the late 1970s the Florida State football team was regularly ranked in the top ten. This was due in part to tremendous coaching from the team's inspirational leader, Bobbie Bowden. Bobbie had a way of instilling confidence in his players by encouraging them in their faith.

During the fall of 1977, Bobbie felt that one of his sophomore players—center Gil Wesley—needed some encouragement. He was hoping Gil would catch the vision of developing a more positive attitude about life and football. To help teach Gil a lesson about "possibility thinking," the coach enlisted his wife's help.

Mrs. Bowden called Gil one evening and said, "Gil, I've got a problem and I really need your help."

Feeling flattered, Gil responded, "Yes, ma'am, how can I help you?"

Mrs. Bowden said, "I'm worried about the coach. Lately he's been despondent about the lack of positive attitude and drive among some of the younger players. He's so upset that he comes home, walks in the door, and without even saying hello to his family, he goes to the tub where he stands and casts into the toilet."

Gil seemed concerned about the coach's mental outlook. "I think the coach has a problem relaxing," he said.

Mrs. Bowden laughed and replied, "No, Gil, his problem isn't relaxing—it's knowing what to do with all the fish he catches."

From that phone call and some follow-up counseling with the coach and his wife, Gil learned the importance of a positive attitude and of remaining faithful in one's endeavors (3 John 5). Gil grasped a new way of looking at life, both on and off the field. He caught the vision of the coach.

I believe we can observe an important parallel with discipleship here. For a disciple to catch a vision, he must first open his heart to the possibilities that exist. If a person has spent his lifetime wearing spiritual blinders, he cannot perceive the divine truths that transform lives. Jesus said, "I have come into this world...so that the blind will see" (John 9:39). Our Lord was addressing His disciples and the Pharisees who suffered from spiritual blindness.

The eyes of the disciples were opened to a new way of life as they observed their Master. They witnessed His miracles and steadily grew in their faith. With the help of Jesus, they began to see the world in a whole new light.

As time passed the disciples came to experience many challenges to their faith that helped shape their vision for ministry and commitment to serve the Lord. It was through these challenges and trials that they learned to unreservedly trust and obey Him.

Admiral William "Bull" Halsey, commander of the American naval fleet during World War II, once said, "There are no great men in this world—only ordinary men who rise to meet great challenges." The common fishermen-disciples learned to rise above their challenges and placed their faith in Jesus. *You and I must do the same.*

Living by Faith

How important is it to live by faith? Turn to your Bible concordance and count the number of passages where Christ is seen to be teaching His disciples about the importance of this virtue. *Faith is crucial.* As the apostle Paul put it in 2 Corinthians 5:7, "We live by faith, not by sight."

But what is faith? Hebrews 11:1 defines faith as "being sure of what we hope for and certain of what we do not see." Commenting on faith, Lawrence Richards, in his *365-Day Devotional* says that "faith is far more than mere hope that something unlikely may happen. It is a deep, internal certainty, rooted in our trust of what God has said."[1]

Now, when Jesus departed from His home in Nazareth and met His disciples at a wedding feast, He gave them very good reason to place their faith in Him—He performed the mighty miracle of turning water into wine. "This, the first of His miraculous signs, Jesus performed at Cana of Galilee. He thus revealed his glory, and His disciples put their faith in him" (John 2:11).

Some time later, as recounted in Matthew 17, we find our Lord challenging the faith of His disciples with several important lessons. Let's take a brief look at these.

As Jesus departed the Sea of Galilee with three of His fishing disciples, He journeyed to a northerly area called Caesarea Philippi. Here He led Peter, James, and John to a mountaintop where He was transfigured before them (Matthew 17:1-2). He pulled back the "veil," so to speak, and let His divine glory shine through in all of its fullness. Here was a clear and visible display of Christ's deity.

Jesus knew the disciples needed to witness His divine power and glory to stretch their faith. We learn elsewhere in Scripture that this display of divine glory made a tremendous impact on the disciples (see 2 Peter 1:16-18).

The group then proceeded to a small village where the disciples had previously visited and ministered. A man approached Jesus and knelt before Him, frustrated because his son had seizures and was suffering greatly (Matthew 17:14-15). The disciples had earlier tried to heal him but did not succeed. Jesus promptly rebuked a demon within the boy and he was healed "from that moment" (verse 18).

The disciples then came to the Master and asked why they were not able to heal the boy (Matthew 17:19). Christ replied, "Because you have so little faith. I tell you the truth, if you have faith as small as a mustard seed, you can say to this mountain, 'Move from here to there' and it will move. Nothing will be impossible for you" (verses 20-21). *Faith is the key*. All they needed was sufficient faith.

Faith and Heavenly Citizenship

It was now time for Jesus to give His disciples a civics lesson—as well as another fishing lesson (Matthew 17:24-27). Besides maturing their faith, Christ helped them to better understand the Christian's role in society as a "model citizen." He taught them about their relationship to the world and its government.

God's wisdom on this important issue is found in several New Testament passages. Foundationally, Scripture reveals that we are citizens of a heavenly kingdom (Philippians 3:20). We are "fellow-citizens with God's people and members of God's household" (Ephesians 2:19).

Because believers are citizens of heaven, they are instructed not to be tainted by the things of this world system. The apostle John captures Christ's teaching on this matter in 1 John 2:15: "Do not love the world or anything in the world. If anyone loves the world, the love of the Father is not in him."

With this as a backdrop, we find Jesus and the disciples confronted with a unique situation in Matthew 17. The publicans were Jews who collected taxes for the temple and the government. They met the disciples as they entered Capernaum and asked, "Doesn't your teacher pay the temple tax?" (Matthew 17:24).

According to custom, every Jew 20 years old and above was required to pay a temple tax. The publicans thus inquired, "Is Jesus above paying the required taxes?"

Peter responded that Jesus does indeed pay the temple tax. Nevertheless, I can see Peter walking back to his home asking himself the question, "Why should Jesus the God-man have to pay taxes?"

As he entered his house, Jesus (knowing what Peter was thinking) said, "What do you think, Simon? From whom do the kings of the earth collect duty and taxes—from their own sons or from others?" "From others," Peter answered. "Then the sons are exempt," Jesus said to him (Matthew 17:25-27).

If anyone *should have* been exempt from a temple tax, it would have been Jesus, the son of God. (Keep in mind that God is the head of the temple. So His son should not have had to pay temple taxes.) This would have been a perfect time for Jesus to say that we are all children of the king, joint heirs of the kingdom, so we do not have to pay taxes.

But what does Jesus say? "So that we may not offend them, go to the lake and throw out your line. Take the first fish you catch; open its mouth and you will find a four-drachma [called a "stater"] coin. Take it and give it to them for my tax and yours" (Matthew 17:27).

Jesus asked Peter to go to the Sea of Galilee, throw out a bare hook, and catch a fish. Peter's faith had grown to the point that he trusted his Master and obeyed His command. With confidence and assurance, this fisherman pitched out a line expecting another wonderful miracle.

Jesus did not have any possessions to pay the taxes. Once again, though, He showed the disciples that He would meet their every need—even payment for the temple tax. Just as Jesus had promised, a fish bit and a large silver coin was inside its mouth.

Today if you visit the Holy Land, you can order a meal of the "Saint Peter's Fish." The fish you will be served is a tilapia or musht. It is a sweet-tasting fish, but rather bony. The locals have several fish farms where these fish are commercially grown.

While this may make good commerce, it is unlikely that this species of fish was the one Peter caught. Of the 18 species of fish in the Sea of Galilee, the most likely candidate would be the barbel or dogfish. It is a carnivore that has a *very large mouth*, similar to a walleye.

In any event, regardless of what species of fish Peter caught, Jesus in this situation again demonstrated that His disciples had very good reason to place their faith in Him. *We do too!* As you and I place our faith in Jesus, He will reach out to meet our needs just as He did for the disciples.

Maturing Our Faith

From Matthew 17 we can glean five key principles based on the experience of the disciples. By applying these principles to our lives, we can stretch our faith while becoming mature disciples.

Honor Christ's Deity

Over the 3½-year ministry of Jesus, He repeatedly demonstrated His deity. The disciples were eyewitnesses of Christ's oneness with God as He was transfigured before them (Matthew 17:2). Jesus continued to provide evidences of His divine power through the many miracles He performed (John 20:30).

When we truly know and study Christ's divine nature and His character, it will have a transforming effect on our lives. Indeed, the more we know God's character, the greater our love will be for Him. The greater our love, the greater our trust will be. And faith will be strengthened as we continue to grow in His wonderful grace.

Rebuke Evildoers

A second principle we can apply in maturing in our faith is to take a stand against evildoers. One way faith manifests itself is by standing against evil—including Satan, the evil one.

The sinful character of this world suggests that we must constantly be on guard against the evil one. The apostle Peter learned this and admonishes us in 1 Peter 5:8-9:

Be self-controlled and alert. Your enemy the devil prowls around like a roaring lion looking for someone to devour. Resist him, standing firm in the faith, because you know that your brothers throughout the world are undergoing the same kind of sufferings.

Jesus recognized the demon in the boy who had seizures, and He cast the evil spirit out (Matthew 17:18). We are instructed, "Submit yourselves, then, to God. Resist the devil, and he will flee from you" (James 4:7). Our faith gives us the power to resist.

Submit to Authority

A third principle that testifies to our faith is that of submitting to authority. Jesus showed the disciples the importance of this principle by acknowledging the taxation right of those who ruled over the land and temple. He encouraged the disciples to submit to those who ruled over them.

This principle was learned well by the disciple Peter. In speaking to other disciples in the first-century church, Peter instructed:

> Keep your behavior excellent among the Gentiles, so that in the thing in which they slander you as evildoers, they may on account of your good deeds, as they observe them, glorify God in the day of visitation. Submit yourselves for the Lord's sake to every human institution, whether to a king as the one in authority, or to governors as sent by him for the punishment of evildoers and the praise of those who do right. (1 Peter 2:12-14 NASB)

We are to obey the law of the land and respect our leaders so we will not be slandered as evildoers. It is important that we not shame the name of our Lord by refusing to be law-abiding citizens.

I asked a friend of mine why he did not place an "icthus" (Christian fish) on his car. He responded, "The way I speed around, I don't want anyone to know I am a Christian."

While I appreciate his desire to avoid being identified with the Lord on this issue, it would be far better for everyone if he were to obey the law.

If we encounter a situation in which a law of the land goes against God's law, however, then our higher obligation is to submit to God's law (see Acts 4:19-20; 5:28-29). With the conviction of the Holy Spirit and the wise counsel of other believers, we should judge whether a specific law of the land is against God's teachings.

For example, in Acts 4 and 5 Peter and the apostles were commanded by governing authorities not to speak publicly about Jesus. They violated this command, for their higher obligation was to follow *Christ's* command to be His witnesses (Matthew 28:19).

I believe that Christ Himself showed His ultimate submission to the authorities when He suffered for the sins of humankind and allowed Himself to be put to death on the cross of Calvary. *Can we submit to others so that through our surrendered hearts we might be seen as modeling Christ's life?*

Be a Good Citizen

A fourth principle we can glean from our study is that we are called to be good citizens. Although Christ was an heir to the God of the temple and should have been exempt from paying taxes, He chose to pay them anyway. He wanted to provide a good role model and witness for others to follow. He did not want anyone to misconstrue a claim of exemption as a claim of indifference.

We honor our Lord by paying our taxes and rendering unto the state that which is due. We need to pay our taxes so that those who account for such things will see that believers are participants and not slackers. Our belief will testify to the ultimate owner of everything. *It is all His!* We testify to our faithfulness by acknowledging that God is the great provider.

Trust in God for Miracles

Finally, a disciple should trust in God for miracles. God

is still in the business of miraculously providing for His children. Unfortunately, many today have come to trust the corporation for their miracles, or perhaps large government, or the high tech society in which we live. All these will ultimately fail us.

Moreover, as precious as our family is to our welfare, even family members at times fail us. King David recognized this as he wrote in Psalm 27: "When my father and my mother forsake me, then the Lord will take me up" (verse 10 KJV). Like David, we must remember that "the Lord is my strength...and He is a saving defense to His anointed" (Psalm 28:7-8 NASB). The Lord is always there for us, and He provides for us today just as He did for the disciples in the first century.

I keep a journal of all God's miracles in our family. In those dark and lonely times when life seems a real burden, I read through this journal of God's faithfulness and provision. Often when we are fearful or despondent in the present, it is helpful to reflect on fulfilled promises of the past. (I think it is wise to keep a journal of fulfilled promises, because Satan does not want us to remember them.)

God's mighty hand has provided miracles in my life that cannot be denied. Let me share a few of them with you.

• When I first started Let's Go Fishing Ministries in 1981, having retired from tournament fishing, God provided additional sponsors when I thought I would lose all my sponsorship.

• That same year I faced a life-threatening surgery. God was faithful and delivered me from the jaws of death.

• In 1986 I wanted to leave a 20-year career in public administration to pursue ministry full-time. To make this possible, God provided several faith partners and a host of volunteer supporters.

• Our twin sons were blessed with outstanding musical ability when they were six years of age. In 1988 God provided a way for them to go to college without totally bankrupting our family. After interviewing with several Christian colleges, Christian Heritage College in El Cajon, California offered Dan and Tom a partial scholarship that enabled them to receive an outstanding education while graduating with top honors.

• In 1992 my dad succumbed to the cancer that had challenged him for two years. I faced a most difficult task—that of preaching at his funeral services and burial. God's grace was delivered right on schedule as I trusted Him to provide the comfort, assurance, strength, and wisdom needed to deliver uplifting messages while bonding our family together.

• I have never worried about retirement because I've always believed our Lord's return is imminent. Several of my board members, however, have been concerned about this and have tried to put something in the budget for this purpose. Over the last two years, though retirement funds were budgeted, I have always seen other ministry needs that seemed more important; therefore, no funds have actually been placed aside for this purpose. This year, though, God provided a partial answer when a longtime supporter donated a piece of property and suggested to the board that at least half the funds be placed into my retirement account. What a blessing!

Truly God is still in the business of making miraculous provisions for His people.

Faith and Obedience

Being a committed disciple requires both faith *and* obedience. Like others, I often fail because I focus on the wind-currents (stresses) of life rather than on God's faithfulness and provision (Matthew 14:22-30). Despite my human frailties, my faith in God's sovereignty is the cornerstone of my life and ministry.

Our friends Pat and Shirley Boone wrote us an encouraging letter in this regard in December 1993: "We hope things are solid and fine with you and your family. You're 'walking on water,' I know that. Shirley and I intend, as long as the Lord makes it possible, to walk along with you. Anybody can fish from the shore." Pat and Shirley recognize the faith it takes to be in ministry. Their encouraging letter caused our faith to stretch even more.

If our faith is constant, we will see God's hand in our lives (see Hebrews 11). Like Peter, we must be willing to obey His Word and trust Him for the results. Even when things do not make much sense, we must be willing to cast our bare hooks into the sea of possibility, expecting a miracle. For Peter, the miracle was a fish with a coin in its mouth to pay the temple tax. To a modern-day disciple, the miracle could be as varied as are the needs.

Our task, regardless of the need, is to simply trust and obey. In his gospel song "Trust and Obey," the great song-writer John H. Sammis put it this way:

When we walk with the Lord, in the light of His
    Word,
        What a glory He sheds on our way.
While we do His good will, He abides with us still,
        And with all who will trust and obey.
Trust and obey, for there's no other way to be happy
    in Jesus,
        Than to trust and obey.
Not a burden we bear, not a sorrow we share,
        But our toil He doth richly repay;
Not a grief nor a loss, not a frown or a cross,
        But is blest if we trust and obey. Trust and obey,
            for there's no other way
To be happy in Jesus, But to trust and obey.[2]

Personal Growth

- What do you think Paul meant in 2 Corinthians 5:7 when he said, "We live by faith, not by sight"?

- How did the disciples' faith grow through the fol-lowing periods?

The "come and see" period (John 1:35–4:46)
The "come and follow Me" period (Mark 1:16–17)
The "come and be with Me" period
    (Matthew 9:37–10:1)
The "remain with Me" period (John 13–17)

Chapter Six

Perseverance
"The Patient Fisherman"

It was a magic fall day in Minnesota. The biting cold air and frigid water stimulated a lot of activity in the northwest fishery.

Mort Bank called his longtime friend and fishing pro, Al Lindner, to ask for a big favor. Bill Holmstead, a very successful businessman, had asked Mort if he could work out a fishing trip with the legendary Lindner.

Mort, Bill, and Al agreed to meet at midday near the launch ramp in Brainerd where the In-Fisherman Headquarters was located. They launched into the upper Mississippi and made their way to a location that was favorable for walleye fishing.

Within a few hours, more than 50 good fish had been boated and everyone was having a great time. But the sun was beginning to set and frost was starting to form on their rods. Everyone agreed they should make just one last cast.

Suddenly Bill yelled, "I think I've got a monster on my line! He feels like a really big one!"

Al was less enthused, however. After about five minutes, he decided Bill must have snagged one of those worthless

giant redhorse fish, similar to a large carp. The fish continued to burrow slowly along the bottom. As the drag paid out
more line, Al could see it was going to be a long battle that
would involve moving their small boat to follow the way-
ward fish. He wondered if it was worth all the fuss.

Al's patience was beginning to wear thin and suggested
to Bill that they break off the "old trash fish" and call it a day.
Bill and Mort would have nothing to do with that sugges-
tion. They asked Al to pick up the anchor and motor up so
they could chase this giant. As the anchor was lifted and the
engine started, the big fish was startled and made a 150-foot
dash upstream.

Though night was fast approaching, the excitement of
the fishermen was growing with every bounce of the rod tip.
It was not long before even Al's excitement began to revive.

After some good coaching from Al, Mort fought the fish
to within 20 feet of the boat. The six-pound mono-line
stretched tight and sang in the cool night air as the fish made
a run to the surface.

As it turned to go back down, Al spotted the classic pad-
dlelike tail, and in a flash recognized that this was no ordinary fish, but a monster pike or muskie. This identification
galvanized everyone's commitment to land this trophy. They
had two major problems—it was getting dark and they did
not have a dip net (a net used for scooping fish).

Al decided this fish was worth the struggle and directed
Mort to back-reel while keeping gentle tension on the fish. Al
motored over to the shore and sent Bill to his car to drive to
a local bait store and buy a large net and a flashlight.

As Bill took off, the fish decided it was time to take
another run—this time to the other side of the river. Al
helped Mort pursue the monster by reminding him that
"good things come to those who wait."

As Al and Mort sat in the dark playing their giant fish,
they saw the headlights of the car return. Bill made his way
down to the water's edge with the net and flashlight just in
the nick of time.

After more than an hour-and-a-half, Al scooped up a beautiful, record-breaking 44-pound/one ounce muskie with a one-quarter ounce walleye jig (lure) in his front lip. The fishermen? They broke the all-time record for persistence and patience.

This is the kind of unique thrill that attracts people to this wonderful sport. Ever since the apostle Peter cast his line into the Sea of Galilee (Matthew 17:27), fishermen have been driven by the adventure and challenge of matching wits with our friends with fins. I recently saw a bumper sticker that summarizes an angler's fixation with fishing: "Fishing isn't a matter of life and death—it's more important than that."

Earlier in the book I noted that fishermen have qualities that make them uniquely suited to be good disciples. Christ delighted in working with fishermen. They have a way of infecting others with their perseverance and passion while sharing techniques and skills that encourage others.

The inner drive and zeal that accomplished fishermen bring to their sport is unparalleled in most other occupations. Like a good fisherman, a dedicated disciple is zealous and eager to share information that will help people catch the vision of the "good news" that brings everlasting life.

Our Minnesota fishermen dramatically demonstrated a perseverance that allowed them to land a special prize. Whether leading or prodding others, tackling life's problems, or contributing to some great cause, *perseverance is crucial to success*. The phrase, "Hang in there baby!" is more than an expression of encouragement—it is good advice for a disciple.

On His second tour through Galilee, Jesus taught His disciples the parable of the sower as a way of encouraging them to persevere. He said "the seed on good soil stands for those with a noble and good heart, who hear the word, retain it, *and by persevering produce a crop*" (Luke 8:15, emphasis added).

Our "stick-to-it-iveness" has a lot to do with getting the right results—*God's results*. Many young Americans at the turn of the twentieth century learned this principle when they memorized this little verse from their *McGuffy's Reader*:

> The fisher who draws in his net too soon,
>   Won't have any fish to sell;
> The child who shuts up his book too soon,
>   Won't learn any lessons well.
> If you would have your learning stay,
>   Be patient—don't learn too fast;
> The man who travels a mile each day,
>   May get around the world at last. [1]

Perseverance Is Driven by Passion

The primary quality that drives perseverance is passion. This is certainly what drove the perseverance of the Minnesota fishermen.

For many of us, however, it's easier to talk about passion than to *find* it—or, having found it, to *maintain* it. A disciple *must* have a passion for his work. Nothing challenges a person more than seeing a believer truly excited about his faith.

Gordon MacDonald, in his encouraging book *Restoring Your Spiritual Passion*, observes that

> Passion—the kind that causes some to excel beyond anyone else—dulls one's sense of fatigue, pain, and the need for pleasure or even well-being. Passion leads some to pay incredible prices to reach a goal of some sort. . . . A passion is necessary in the performance of Christian faith. [2]

This kind of passion is illustrated in the life of the apostle Paul. Indeed, Paul spoke from a wellspring of passion when he wrote, "But one thing I do: Forgetting what is behind and straining towards what is ahead, I press on towards the goal to win the prize for which God has called me heavenwards in Christ Jesus" (Philippians 3:13-14).

Many of us experience spiritual passion when we first

receive Christ into our hearts by faith. Like the healed man on the steps at the temple in Jerusalem (Acts 3:8), we leap for joy and are utterly unconcerned about what others may think. Our infectious zeal embarrasses those who have more experience in matters of faith.

As time sets in, some believers overinstitutionalize their faith and spend too much time identifying with folks who have lost the joy of their salvation. If we are not careful, we end up like many one-dimensional Christians—*boring and uncaring.* Too often, we become inactive participants—mere spectators of life around us.

A mature Christian does not preclude passion but learns to control or channel his emotions in a rational manner. He uses his passion as an engine to push his spiritual boat and to encourage others in their faith.

Maintaining Passion in the Face of the Urgent

Most believers go through periods in which they find themselves lacking spiritual passion to one degree or another. We live in a hurried, stress-filled environment that tends to drain us of positive emotions. The busyness of our lifestyle absorbs what passion might exist. We find ourselves investing all our precious energies into events and programs of the "public world."

Meanwhile, our "private world"—the heart—starves for attention and encouragement. The more emphasis we place on *activities,* the less time we have for *devotion.* As MacDonald correctly observes, "Doing more FOR God may mean less time WITH God. Talking becomes an effective substitute for meditating or listening." [3]

Didn't Christ live a pressurized life? He only had about three-and-a-half years to minister before He was taken away. But He never succumbed to the tyranny of the urgent. J. B. Phillips, in his book *Your God Is Too Small,* states,

> It is refreshing and salutary to study the poise and quietness of Christ. His task and responsibility

might well have driven a man out of his mind, but He was never in a hurry, never impressed by numbers, never a slave of the clock. He was acting, He said, as He observed God to act—never in a hurry. [4]

Throughout the gospels, we witness Christ withdrawing from the multitudes to be alone with the Father (Luke 5:16). He regularly recharged His spiritual batteries through prayer and meditation. While being driven by His passion and mission "to seek and to save what was lost" (Luke 19:10), He was guided by a prudent spirit of control and internal balance.

Perhaps this is the model John Wesley (1703-1791) used in balancing his work within reasonable limits. Wesley concluded, "Though I am always in haste, I am never in a hurry because I never undertake more work than I can go through with calmness of spirit."[5] We would be wise to imitate Wesley's modus operandi.

A Growing Passion for Christ

The disciples found the call of the Galilean carpenter to be irresistible. Once the fishermen met the Savior, the everyday task of setting nets became drudgery. They had always enjoyed their work and found it fulfilling. But now the fish began to stink, the mending of nets seemed trivial, and the hours of waiting in the boats became unbearable.

They found their minds traveling back to fellowship around a campfire or Bible study at the feet of the Master. As they experienced more of Christ, their passion for challenging others with "the call" became all-consuming. They had a vision for reaching the world, not just Judea and Samaria.

To be sure, there were times when the disciples—like each of us—became discouraged and waned in their passion and vision. One such occasion was immediately after the Crucifixion.

In John 21 we find Simon Peter and the other disciples at a point of physical and mental exhaustion. They witnessed their leader killed and were forced to endure all the stress-filled events surrounding His death. Judas' betrayal of the Lord (Matthew 26:47-56), Peter's threefold denial of Christ (verses 69-75), and the subsequent trial (27:11-32) had left the disciples without hope or passion. And because they were without passion, their perseverance waned.

In their discouragement, they did the only thing they knew how to do—*they went fishing*. But even as they were fishing, the risen Jesus gloriously appeared and caught their attention on the Sea of Galilee (John 21:1-11). He encouraged them and reshaped their thinking by helping them to refocus their vision for ministry and their calling. *They were to be fishers of men.*

Jesus instructed them, "Go and make disciples of all nations, baptizing them in the name of the Father and of the Son and of the Holy Spirit, and teaching them to obey everything I have commanded you" (Matthew 28:19-20).

Christ restored and reenergized the disciples' spiritual passion. And as their passion was fanned back into a flame, so their will to persevere was renewed within them. They were now ready to face any challenge, knowing that the risen Christ would be with them always.

Poised for Action

Of course, merely knowing about the need to have passion and a vision is not enough. One must be willing to *apply* the lessons learned and *actively participate* in the discipling process.

I am reminded of Jimmy Houston, a man admired by many for his outstanding fishing skills. Folks have studied his techniques and watched his fishing shows every Saturday morning for the past 18 years. Most fishermen know of his philosophy and his strategies. However, one must pick up a rod and bait to *apply* what is learned in a real-life situation. Having the right attitude alone is not enough. *One must be willing to commit oneself to the challenge of fishing.*

That is what the discipling process is all about—getting

involved, being passionate about our calling, and being persistent in applying all we know.

Personal Growth

- Three conditions for discipleship are identified in the Gospel of John. List them below.

    John 8:31 _____

    John 13:35 _____

    John 15:8 _____

- Would you say you persevere well under pressure?

- How much passion do you have for the things of God?

- List three things you could do to enhance your spiritual passion.

    1._____

    2._____

    3._____

Proper Attitude and Equipment
"The Call to Fish"

People enjoy fishing in a wide variety of ways. For some, sitting on a bucket with a long cane pole fishing for bluegill is an enjoyable way to spend a day. For others, speeding across a calm lake at 70 miles per hour in a low-profile, tournament bass boat provides excitement. For still others, wading a pristine stream in a wilderness area with an 8½-foot dry-fly rod looking for that elusive brown trout is what fishing is all about.

Over my lifetime, I have had the privilege of encouraging over two million people on the joys of fishing. While most of the instruction has been directed toward general freshwater fishing, I have spent considerable time encouraging others in specialty areas such as light saltwater and tournament black bass fishing.

Regardless of the type of fishing, there are some basic principles and traits that all master fishermen share. Without a proper appreciation for each of these qualities, a fisherman will find himself lacking in the knowledge and the skill necessary to be consistently productive.

Christ knew these traits and qualities were the same

characteristics needed to be an effective disciple. That is why He chose eight fishermen to be among His first 12 disciples.

In this book I have drawn an analogy between fishing and discipling. I see the fisherman in this analogy as a disciple (or believer). The fish is equivalent to the person who is lost—a person without Christ. The rod and reel may be likened to spiritual gifts—the equipment God gives His disciples. The line connecting the rod and reel to the lure is the Holy Spirit. Our many lures are the various testimonies and experiences God has given each of us.

Unlike fishing for fish, we do not seek to fish for souls so we can boast about the size and weight of our stringers. Nor should we measure the effectiveness of our ministry by the number of "fish caught," but by how we relate and connect with the lost on a daily basis.

The ultimate fisherman is a tournament professional who possesses certain qualities that enable him to be extremely effective in his work. In like manner, the committed disciple must possess certain skills and abilities to be a good fisherman for our Lord.

It is important for both fishermen and disciples to be properly prepared for the challenges and opportunities facing them. They must be able to adapt and react to the changing environment by properly preparing themselves with the right attitude, knowledge, and patience. Because these qualities are so important, let's look at them in more detail.

The Right Attitude

A tournament fisherman develops a positive strategy and competitive desire to encourage both himself and his team on to victory. He must maintain a quiet confidence with every cast, believing that if the bait is worked correctly, he will successfully stimulate the fish to bite.

Related to this, I think it is amazing to witness how excited fishermen can become when they find a new lure or product that creates excitement with the fish. They tell everyone they meet about "the good news" of their product discovery and how it is making an impact on the fishery.

A disciple needs the same positive, affirming, and even competitive attitude to be an encouragement to the unbeliever. We must be excited about the "product" we have to share—*the gospel that leads to eternal life*. Isn't it an embarrassment that the greatest news of all—eternal life through God's Son—should be kept a secret by so many of His disciples?

Ephesians 4:23 indicates that a proper attitude comes from the Holy Spirit and by studying God's Word. Believers are encouraged "to be *made new* in the attitude of your minds" (emphasis added). The attributes of confidence and unselfishness are to be woven into the fabric of our character.

Scripture also tells us that we are to model the attitude of Christ in our daily lives (Philippians 2:5). Indeed, we are to focus our minds on "whatever is true, whatever is noble, whatever is right, whatever is pure, whatever is lovely, whatever is admirable—if anything is excellent or praiseworthy— think about such things" (4:8). For a disciple, it is *imperative* that we have an open and loving heart that manifests itself with an infectious attitude that attracts people to the Christ who is working in and through us.

Acting on Knowledge

A seasoned angler studies various techniques and theories that can be used in improving his stringer. Every day new scientific discoveries come to light that help him to better understand the nature, character, and environment of fish. A good fisherman studies all available information and applies it to each given fishing situation.

Only a foolish and prideful fisherman or disciple ignores the quest to discover new truths. Solomon once said, "Every prudent man acts out of knowledge, but a fool exposes his folly" (Proverbs 13:16). A discerning heart will seek knowledge in order to become equipped for service (Proverbs 15:14). A committed disciple will call out as the psalmist did, "Teach me knowledge and good judgment" (Psalm 119:66).

A disciple prepares himself by studying the Word of God, while continually exploring new ways to present the truth.

The Bible has the answer to virtually every question we can ask. We are encouraged to ask of God when we lack wisdom, for our Lord "gives to all men generously and without reproach" (James 1:5 NASB).

Prior to being martyred during the reign of the Roman emperor Nero, Peter penned these encouraging words to his disciples: "But grow in the grace and knowledge of our Lord and Savior Jesus Christ. To him be the glory both now and forever" (2 Peter 3:18).

Maintaining Patience

One of my favorite fishing stories relates to a trip I took in the California delta. An aspiring young pro had asked me to accompany him on a half-day trip. The pro was seeking to utilize my background and experience on the delta as a guide to help him become a more effective fisherman.

After checking out a couple of my favorite spots, we boated along for another mile. In front of us was an old sunken barge probably 45 feet long. This wooden relic had been submerged since World War II when many of the abandoned ammunition barges were discarded in the delta.

Over the course of many years, barnacles and crustaceans had built up on the boat, thereby attracting many forage fish to the area. I believed the barge had to hold fish because there was no other good-looking structure within a mile.

As we spent some time pitching our plastic crawfish and worms down the length of this barge, I was shocked that we did not receive any bites. As we got to the end, though, I decided to recast into an area where both of us had just worked. This time I waited a little longer before retrieving my lure. As I retrieved it, I shook my rod tip, thereby transmitting tremors onto the lure.

Suddenly, I felt that notorious thud and reared back to hook a nice three-pounder. My partner could not believe I caught the fish in the area we had just worked. I turned the boat and quickly motored back up to the beginning of the barge where we first started.

With a puzzled look, my partner asked, "Why are we recasting in the same water we just fished?" I suggested that we hadn't properly fished the water because we had been short of patience with every cast.

As we continued fishing that wreck, we picked up another five fish. Demonstrating more patience by working the bait slower was just what was needed.

A good fisherman knows that sometimes he must throw to the same spot several times before the fish will strike. Repeated presentations, using different lures and techniques, will often cause even the most stubborn and wary fish to finally become interested.

So often disciples make a single feeble attempt to share truth with a friend or neighbor and then become discouraged because their message was not initially received well. We quickly become disappointed with those who seem disinterested in God's Word.

This is especially the case when we share our faith with relatives or close friends. It is admittedly difficult to discuss matters of spiritual significance with those who are closest to us. We often make the excuse that "we tried once and have fulfilled our discipleship duties." *But have we?* Did we persevere *with patience*?

The apostle James reminds us that those who persevere with patience yield results in the end (James 1:12). As disciples we should always be patient as we approach each challenge and opportunity.

The Right Equipment

In preparing for a day's fishing, a master fisherman thoughtfully selects the necessary equipment for his trip. Careful attention is given to details. Only equipment that is clean and operating efficiently will be selected. This minimizes the potential for disruption or frustration due to equipment failure.

The most important equipment a fisherman needs is his rod and reel, the fishing line, and a good assortment of tackle. Without these basic tools, he would find fishing very frustrating if not impossible.

Just as a fisherman needs the right equipment to fish, so a disciple must have the right "equipment" for the specific task God has set before him. In what follows, we shall draw some analogies between the fisherman's equipment and that used by the disciple.

Rod and Reel (Spiritual Gifts and Natural Talents)

The rod and reel are very important to the success of a fisherman. The make or quality of the gear is not nearly as important as knowing how to use each item effectively.

A rod must be sensitive enough to feel the light bite of a timid fish while sturdy enough in the butt section to set the hook into the jaw of the fish. Selection of a rod should be based on the species one is attempting to catch and the type of fishing one wishes to pursue.

My favorite way to catch a fish is by using an ultralight rod with a fast taper action that enables me to have *both* the needed sensitivity *and* the strength to work effectively. Despite the size, though, the most important thing is that the rod and reel be properly balanced with the line, lures, and angler's level of competence.

Just as there are different types of rod and reel combinations, so there are a variety of spiritual gifts. "There are different kinds of gifts but the same spirit," the apostle Paul tells us (1 Corinthians 12:4). Each of us "have different gifts, according to the grace given us" (Romans 12:6). These gifts include serving, teaching, encouraging, contributing to the needs of others, leadership, and showing mercy (Romans 12:6-8). Other gifts are listed in 1 Corinthians 12:1-11.

We need *all* the spiritual gifts in order to function as an effective body of believers. Our gifts are to be used as "functioning equipment" that can enable the Holy Spirit to work within and through us.

Regardless of what spiritual gifts we may have, *all* our gifts are to be used in honoring and serving our Lord. As the apostle Peter put it, "Each one should use whatever gift he has received to serve others, faithfully administering God's grace in its various forms" (1 Peter 4:10).

God has also given each of us specific talents. *In what areas are you talented?* God can use these areas for His glory.

What are some areas of interest, hobbies, vocations, avocations, struggles, victories, afflictions, and healings that are unique to you? Did you ever stop to think that God can use you in reaching others who share your circumstances, experiences, and ambitions? *He can!*

If we are to be truly effective disciples, we must meet people in the marketplace of life and use our spiritual gifts *and* our talents to share the greatest news of all—*salvation in Jesus Christ.*

Fishing Line (the Holy Spirit)

It is imperative that a master fisherman continually check and restore his fishing line. The line is the vital link between the rod and reel and the lures.

There are a variety of lines, and the quality varies with the cost of the product. It is important to always have enough good line on your reel to provide the best possible chance of catching that fish of a lifetime.

Most major manufacturers produce fishing lines that are abrasive-resistant and minimize line stretch. These are important factors that affect the setting action on the fish. Line should be frequently checked and replaced—particularly after heavy use or fishing around abrasive objects such as trees, rocks, and brush.

As a fisherman depends on good line, so a disciple depends on the Holy Spirit. A disciple must constantly walk in dependence upon the Holy Spirit for guidance, direction, and wisdom (Galatians 5:16). The Holy Spirit is a divine enabler who empowers us to use our gifts (rods and reels) and testimonies (lures) effectively as we interrelate with others.

John the Baptist prophesied that Jesus would come and baptize with the Holy Spirit (Luke 3:16). This was ultimately fulfilled on the day of Pentecost (Acts 2). Since that time every believer experiences the baptism of the Holy Spirit (1 Corinthians 12:13).

Prior to sending out His disciples, Christ spoke of the importance of the Holy Spirit as an encourager and teacher: "The Counselor, the Holy Spirit, whom the Father will send in my name, will teach you all things and will remind you of everything I have said to you" (John 14:26).

A disciple-fisherman needs to be filled regularly with the Holy Spirit (Ephesians 5:18). The daily challenges of life are sometimes abrasive and demanding to our supply of the Spirit. Through ministering to others we periodically empty our spool of resources and need to be refilled with the fresh Spirit so that we can continue to serve our Lord.

Your life cannot be sustained without renewal from God. It is essential to replace the body's energy by eating, sleeping, and exercising. Similarly, the Christian cannot function without his soul being revitalized by reading God's Word (as illuminated by the Holy Spirit), listening to spirit-filled Bible teaching, and by participating in the soul-filling table of Communion. The prophet Isaiah urges, "Let the people renew their strength" (Isaiah 41:1 KJV).

Part of revitalizing our lives involves taking time to be still and listening to God (Psalm 46:10). In humble prayer, draw near to the footstool of His divine mercy, and realize the fulfillment of His promise: "Those who wait for the Lord will gain new strength" (Isaiah 40:31 NASB). He will always hold us as the object of His infinite affection and encouragement.

The Tackle Box and the Lures
(Our Testimonies and Life Experiences)

A good fisherman will have different baits and lures that can be used to catch a variety of fish in different situations. Each fisherman has his favorite lures and will most effectively use these when fishing difficult situations. Each lure has a specific purpose and can be selected according to its particular effectiveness.

By analogy, we might liken the tackle box and assorted lures to our personal testimonies. Those intimate, life-changing experiences and memories help equip us to share the personal relationship we enjoy with the Lord with others. Just as good bait attracts a fish, so we can attract unbelievers to the Lord by our vibrant testimonies.

Each day brings new opportunities for the Lord to do His miracles and to build memories in our lives that will encourage us and others in our spiritual journeys. Life's experiences provide all of us unique snapshots that can be shared with others. Truly there is power in a vibrant testimony (Revelation 12:11).

The Last Cast

Upon Christ's resurrection and appearance to the 11 disciples, He issued the Great Commission to them along the same shoreline where He first met them. He said, "All authority in heaven and on earth has been given to me. Therefore go and make disciples of all nations, baptizing them in the name of the Father and of the Son and of the Holy Spirit, and teaching them to obey everything I have commanded you" (Matthew 28:18-20).

I am sure most Christans have heard or read the Great Commission many times. Yet, it is surprising how many of them are still standing on the shore, watching others fish. Perhaps some feel their equipment is not good enough? Have we forgotten *who issues* the equipment?

Many believe this work should be left to the real pros—pastors, priests, missionaries, and church workers. But the Great Commission was written to *all* Christians.

James, the half-brother of Jesus, reminds us, "Prove yourselves doers of the word, and not merely hearers who delude themselves" (James 1:22). If we are going to be "doers" of the Word, we must participate in fulfilling the Great Commission.

Of course, there are some who feel that the "fish" might not be interested. However, God promises that His Word will not return void (Isaiah 55:10-11). A disciple serious about his call realizes that there exists in each person a spiritual vacuum—an empty spirit crying out for God. People are seeking meaning and purpose in life. The reality is that the "fish" are very hungry. Our concern, then, is more a question of *how* and *when* we present the Word in a way they can understand.

In his book *Jesus Christ, Disciple Maker*, Bill Hull suggests,

> When Jesus calls a person, he calls him to a purpose, a dream, a goal, a life-changing vision. The vision is to be a fisher of men. These Galilean men (disciples) understood fishing, and they were certainly acquainted with the lost state of men. Therefore, the call to fish for men turned their heads; their hearts were aflame for it! [1]

When you stop and think about it, there are people you see every day who will never see Jesus in anyone but you. They may have never entered a church, gone to a Bible study, or watched an evangelistic television program. That is why we need to understand the importance of using our gifts and our talents to be fishers of men.

It's time to go fishing!

Personal Growth

- How have you prepared your heart and soul to serve the Lord (Psalm 51:10)?

- Have you carefully analyzed your spiritual gifts? How are you using them?

- What unique testimonies and experiences has God given you to share with others?

- How is fishing for men similar to fishing for fish?

Chapter Eight

Overcoming Obstacles
"Big Bad Sharks"

In our two-engine chartered plane, we were rapidly descending through thick clouds at 200 miles per hour. The majestic mountain peaks of the Alaskan Range—including the great Mount McKinley at 20,320 feet—pushed through the cloud cover like shark's teeth in a sea of foam.

Our approach was dropping us into a canyon that contained the chilly waters of Lake Iliamna. If everything worked the way it was planned, we would come out of the clouds 500 feet above the middle of the lake.

The wings of the plane began to chatter in the icy air as the plane descended from the sky. The plane fluttered in the turbulence as my fishing buddies strained to see...*anything*... through the white mist surrounding us.

Casual conversation stopped and rapid breathing took its place. In a matter of seconds, the emotion of fear became our in-flight companion.

Fear penetrates the heart with questions of doubt and mistrust of the unknown and the unseen. Even the combat-hardened Vietnam War vet traveling with us began to feel the essence of fear that consumed the cockpit as perspiration began to flow freely.

Fear can captivate people like a man-eating shark imbedding its sharp teeth into soft flesh. It can rip and tear away hunks of faith and inner peace from the body of life. When such fear strikes, atheists suddenly seek the comfort of the Creator and saints began to confess their sins.

Fear. Have you ever wrestled with it? It creeps into our lives without regard to position, power, or authority. There are all kinds of fears—fear of heights, fear of flying, fear of rejection, fear of crowds, fear of the dark, fear of being alone, fear of financial failure, fear of dying, and much more. Maybe you have experienced one of these foes.

Fear can grip us in ways that often seem merciless. If we allow it to consume us, fear can rob us of our effectiveness. Our spiritual might can be turned into quivering flesh once fear and doubt close their tight jaws on our lives.

Disciples Are Not Exempt from Fear

Disciples are not exempt from the pain of fear. I recall a story from my good friend, Al Lindner, that helps us better understand the power of fear. I have known Al for well over a dozen years and have found him to be a truly authentic disciple.

In 1980, after struggling with his spiritual and personal life for a number of years, Al, who is the President of In-Fisherman Communications Network, dedicated his life *and* his company to Jesus Christ. His lifestyle changed as did the direction of In-Fisherman. There was a new commitment to excellence and innovation that continues to guide this outstanding media corporation today.

As a way of acknowledging Christ, all their publications and television programs proudly display a gold cross superimposed on top of an "icthus"—the secret sign first used by the disciples to identify allegiance to Christ. In the Greek the five letters of "fish" (i-ch-th-u-s) also stand for "Jesus Christ—Son of God, Savior."

In 1988 the In-Fisherman Corporation started the Professional Walleye Circuit which sponsors major tournaments similar to the famous Bassmaster Tour. As a part of their program, Al instituted a FOCAS (Fellowship of Christian Angler's Society) prayer meeting for any interested participants. This meeting provided an opportunity for Christian fellowship with others interested in sharing their concerns and growing in their faith.

Due to the rigorous travel schedule on the tournament trail, many pros are rarely able to attend their home churches. The FOCAS meetings can be a real encouragement to all who attend.

In-Fisherman was holding a late summer tournament on Lake Huron. Just before most of the anglers started heading back to the weigh-in station, a tremendous storm moved in that produced life-threatening conditions.

Through a series of misunderstandings, the check-in boat attendant inadvertently crossed off "Boat Number 31," which in fact had not checked in. The wind and waves had already taken their toll with over 20 boats badly broken up but nevertheless safely in port.

Following the weigh-in ceremonies, Al and his staff were leaving the parking lot and saw an empty trailer. They realized there must be one more boat still out in the storm.

They immediately alerted the Coast Guard and the next of kin of the missing anglers. The question everyone pondered was, "How could the fishermen possibly survive this ordeal?"

Al later learned that the fishermen had patched the hull of their old boat to make it seaworthy for this tournament. Recognizing the approaching storm, they tried to make a run to shore only to discover that the unforgiving lake had ripped apart their patch.

As the lake water began to fill the boat, the batteries shorted out, thereby eliminating the use of either their lights or their UHF emergency radio. As they tried to guide the water-laden boat toward shore, they soon ran out of gas and were pushed about 40 miles from shore into the dark, stormy night.

Hanging onto the boat for dear life, they knew their only hope was that someone would realize they were missing and start a rescue search. They hung onto their emergency flare, waiting for the opportunity to signal their rescuers.

Finally, at about three o'clock in the morning, a coast guard helicopter passed overhead. The fishermen ripped open their flare only to find it was totally waterlogged and unusable.

Back at the tournament headquarters, Al organized a prayer team that stayed up all night "locked in prayer." These dedicated competitors laid aside their differences and committed themselves to fervent intercession.

In that little room where a handful of anglers knelt to intercede on behalf of their fellow fishermen, *miracles began to happen.* These rugged mountain men from Canada and the northern states began to sense God's presence. They began to feel His peace and comfort while experiencing the tender side of one another.

Early the next morning, a massive search was initiated. Within a few hours, the two lost fishermen were found still clinging to their boat, using it as a life preserver. They were in hypothermia and in shock—*but were nevertheless alive.*

God answered the prayers of those faithful fishermen who had gathered and prayed for a miracle. Who won or lost the tournament was no longer important. Those who witnessed God's presence in that little prayer room received a trophy that would not ever rust or be taken away. Their expanded faith in Christ was the reward that would see them through life. A new slogan became a part of the Walleye Circuit: "Lock it in prayer."

Stormy Water Adventures in Jesus' Time

On two separate occasions, Jesus used the stormy waters of the Sea of Galilee to remind His disciples of the lessons taught in David's 27th Psalm. This psalm contains a potent repellent to the "shark attacks" of fear—"Whom shall I fear? The Lord is the stronghold of my life—of whom shall I be afraid" (verse 1).

In Mark 6:45-51, we find the disciples returning before nightfall from the miraculous feeding of 5,000 people, and Jesus bids them to go back:

> Immediately Jesus made his disciples get into the boat and go on ahead of him to Bethsaida, while he dismissed the crowd. After leaving them, he went up on a mountainside to pray.
>
> When evening came, the boat was in the middle of the lake, and he was alone on land. He saw the disciples straining at the oars, because the wind was against them. About the fourth watch of the night, he went out to them, walking on the lake. He was about to pass by them, but when they saw him walking on the lake, they thought he was a ghost. They cried out, because they all saw him and were terrified.
>
> Immediately he spoke to them and said, "Take courage! It is I. Don't be afraid." Then he climbed into the boat with them, and the wind died down. They were completely amazed.

On another occasion, we find Jesus along with Peter and his fishing friends crossing the lake. Again, a winter evening storm emerged and assaulted the disciples—this time while boating from Capernaum to Kursi located on the eastern shore:

> Without warning, a furious storm came up on the lake, so that the waves swept over the boat. But Jesus was sleeping. The disciples went and woke him, saying, "Lord, save us! We're going to drown!"
>
> He replied, "You of little faith, why are you so afraid?" Then he got up and rebuked the winds and the waves, and it was completely calm.
>
> The men were amazed and asked, "What kind of man is this? Even the winds and the waves obey him!" (Matthew 8:24-27)

Today's Galilean fishermen tell us such storms on the Kinnereth are common during the winter. These well-known eastern storms—called *Sharkia* in Arabic (shark)—have always caused apprehension among fishermen according to historians.

Christ used these "stormy water adventures" to establish and increase the disciples' faith in His deity. When the disciples asked the rhetorical question in Matthew 8:27—"What kind of man is this?"—they were acknowledging Christ's deity and power. Although miracles are hard for modern man to accept, the New Testament is clear that Jesus is Lord, not only over His church, but also over all creation. The disciples recognized that because Christ could control the realm of nature, He was God.

What can we learn from these stormy water adventures of the disciples? What wisdom can we glean from these stories on how we should approach fear? Consider the following.

Fear Develops Faith and Character

Fear can help develop both faith and character in the life of a Christian. Let me illustrate this with a fish story.

As Easterners transplanted themselves to the West Coast, they found themselves longing for the East Coast cod. It was often shipped by rail to several fine dining restaurants on the West Coast. The customers, though, complained that the fish just weren't the same. Despite providing aerated containers with water from the original source, the fish arrived soft and tasteless.

Then someone reckoned that the fish needed to be challenged in a real-life environment. Catfish or bullheads were among the natural predators of the cods and were introduced into the shipping containers. From that time forward, the fish arrived firm and tasty.

Life without some stress presents no challenges to mature our faith and firm up our convictions. Real living involves dealing with the catfish of life. It is healthy for us to encounter people and circumstances that challenge us and refine our character.

Through these challenges, we are able to test our faith and witness God's miracles. The raging waters of our lives will be calmed as we rest in God's sovereign hands. If we focus on the Lord and His promises, we will not be robbed of joy in our lives, despite the circumstances.

Popular writer Chuck Swindoll tells us that worry, stress, and fear can be joy stealers. Listen to his words:

> Worry is an inordinate anxiety about something that may or may not occur. It has been my observation that what is being worried about usually does not occur. But worry eats away at joy like slow-working acid while we are waiting for the outcome.
>
> Stress is a little more acute than worry. Stress is intense strain over a situation we cannot change or control—something beyond our control, and instead of releasing it to God, we churn over it. It is in that restless churning stage that our stress is intensified. Usually the thing that plagues us is not as severe as we make it out to be.
>
> Fear, on the other hand, is different from worry and stress. It is dreadful uneasiness over the presence of danger, evil, or pain. As with the other two, however, fear usually makes things appear worse than they really are.[1]

We need to keep things in perspective. If we focus on our fears, they always appear bigger and worse than they really are. But if we focus on God's sovereign control, fear is kept in check and God uses our experiences to mature our faith.

Faith Dispels Fear

Faith can dispel fear, but only in proportion to its strength. As the faith of the disciples grew, their strength to overcome their fears also increased.

We need to relax in the promises Christ gave His first-century disciples. During His farewell discourse prior to His betrayal, Jesus comforted His disciples by saying, "Do not let your hearts be troubled. Trust in God; trust also in me" (John 14:1). Moreover, Jesus said, "Peace I leave with you; my peace I give you. I do not give to you as the world gives. Do not let your hearts be troubled and do not be afraid" (verse 27).

The disciples' belief in these wonderful promises allowed them to mature in their faith. They were able to declare their assurance in Christ and victory over fear in their ministries.

Following are some verses that are especially helpful for those confronting fear:

• "For God did not give us a spirit of timidity, but a spirit of power, of love and of self-discipline" (2 Timothy 1:7).

• "So we say with confidence, 'The Lord is my helper; I will not be afraid. What can man do to me?' " (Hebrews 13:6).

• "For you did not receive a spirit that makes you a slave again to fear, but you received the Spirit of sonship. And by him we cry, 'Abba, Father' " (Romans 8:15).

• "There is no fear in love. But perfect love drives out fear, because fear has to do with punishment. The one who fears is not made perfect in love" (1 John 4:18).

God's Recipe for Dealing with "Shark Attacks"

One of the best recipes for attacking fear can be found in David's 27th Psalm. David's numerous struggles with fearful situations qualify him to be a "wise counselor" to all of us. Consider his words:

> The Lord is my light and my salvation—
>   whom shall I fear?
> The Lord is the stronghold of my life—
>   of whom shall I be afraid?
> When evil men advance against me
>   to devour my flesh,
> when my enemies and my foes attack me,
>   they will stumble and fall.

Though an army besiege me,
    my heart will not fear;
though war break out against me, even then will
    I be confident.
One thing I ask of the Lord, this is what I seek:
that I may dwell in the house of the Lord
    all the days of my life,
to gaze upon the beauty of the Lord
    and to seek himin his temple.
For in the day of trouble he will keep me safe
    in his dwelling;
he will hide me in the shelter of his tabernacle
    and set me high upon a rock.
Then my head will be exalted above the enemies
    who surround me;
at his tabernacle will I sacrifice with shouts of joy;
    I will sing and make music to the Lord.
Hear my voice when I call, O Lord; be merciful
    to me and answer me.
My heart says of you, "Seek his face!"
    Your face, Lord, I will seek.
Do not hide your face from me,
    do not turn your servant away in anger;
    you have been my helper.
Do not reject me or forsake me, O God my Savior.
Though my father and mother forsake me,
    the Lord will receive me.
Teach me your way, O Lord; lead me in a straight
    path because of my oppressors.
Do not hand me over to the desire of my foes,
    for false witnesses rise up against me,
    breathing out violence.
I am still confident of this: I will see the goodness
    of the Lord in the land of the living.
Wait for the Lord; be strong and take heart
    and wait for the Lord.

This psalm is virtually brimming with spiritual gems. To summarize David's eloquent expressions, we can sift the following truths that can be used to fight off attacks of fear:

• *Seek God's Protection:* "He will keep me safe...he will hide me in the shelter of his tabernacle and set me high upon a rock" (verse 5).

• *Worship God's Majesty:* "I will sing and make music to the Lord" (verse 6).

• *Prayer:* "Hear my voice when I call, O Lord; be merciful to me and answer me" (verse 7).

• *Focus on the Lord:* "Your face, Lord, I will seek" (verse 8).

• *Study God's Word:* "Teach me your way, O Lord; lead me in a straight path" (verse 11).

• *Be Confident:* "I am still confident of this: I will see the goodness of the Lord" (verse 13).

• *Be Patient:* "Wait for the Lord" (verse 14).

• *Be Courageous:* "Be strong and take heart" (verse 14).

A disciple will strive to "lock up his fears in prayer." This is what fisherman Al Lindner did when some of his fishermen friends were lost in a storm. This is what David did when faced with vicious enemies. This is what you and I must do.

Fear not—He is with you always. The Lord is the stronghold of your life!

Personal Growth

• What are three fears that try to rob you of a joyful life?

  _____

  _____

  _____

• How is God bigger than your fears?

- Read God's comforting Word to help you overcome your fears (2 Timothy 1:7; Romans 8:15; 1 John 4:18; Psalm 91:1; Psalm 27:2; Isaiah 51:12-16).

- Will you try "locking up your fears in prayer"?

Discouragement
"Tough Days—Empty Livewells"

It has always been curious to watch tournament fishermen at the final weigh-ins. Some purposely show up at the very last second and motor slowly around the entire marina hoping someone will ask them how they did.

These show-offs are full of fish stories as they reach into their livewells and hold up their trophies for all to behold. You can see the anticipation as they wait their turn to confront the scales and the curious onlookers. As they "politely" allow others to weigh-in before them, there is a sense of boastfulness and pride as they finally motor to the weigh-in station.

These pretentious fishermen deliberately fumble around, retrieving their fish from their livewells as everyone looks on. As they swagger to the podium, they look out upon the crowd with a Cheshire-cat grin as if to say, *in your face*. Most of the onlookers bite into the feelings of despair and inferiority that accompany a heart that lusts after something someone else has.

It is the same feeling one gets in the south when one motors by some brim fishermen who are having the day of a lifetime. Standing near the fish cleaning table at the end of the day, one will likely hear the fishermen describe their experience this way: "Jim-Bob and I launched our boat at dawn and we didn't see our bobbers for more than 15 minutes all day long."

Then there are those fishermen whose livewells are empty and they look for a place to escape. As others are weighing in, you can see a few boats sneak away from the group and move toward the launch ramp. Their livewells are empty and so are their spirits.

While others have succeeded and earned the right to at least make an appearance before the crowd, these forsaken anglers wonder why the "fish gods" failed to look down upon them this day. They begin to question their abilities and decisions. Suddenly those golf clubs they sold at the garage sale a few years back look pretty good.

God Mends Broken Hearts

Sometimes we learn the most about ourselves and others during times when things are toughest. I often teach folks that those days when fishing is the hardest—the days when it seems like all the fish in the lake have been raptured—is when you learn the most. That is when you apply various techniques and new skills to try to stretch your understanding of the sport to the limit.

Life is a lot like fishing. There are those struggles and defeats that challenge us to the very limit. When things do not go our way, that is when we learn a lot about ourselves and our loving God.

I believe God does His best work when we present ourselves to Him, broken and defeated. At these times we place our total faith in Him. When we are at the end of our rope and willing to release control, God can step in and direct our lives.

At the outset of His ministry, Jesus quoted Isaiah 61:1-3 to describe why He (the promised Messiah) came:

> The Spirit of the Sovereign LORD is on me, because the LORD has anointed me to preach good

news to the poor. He has sent me to bind up the brokenhearted, to proclaim freedom for the captives and release from darkness for the prisoners, to proclaim the year of the LORD's favor and the day of vengeance of our God, to comfort all who mourn, and provide for those who grieve in Zion—to bestow on them a crown of beauty instead of ashes, the oil of gladness instead of mourning, and a garment of praise instead of a spirit of despair. They will be called oaks of righteousness, a planting of the LORD for the display of his splendor.

"Brokenhearted," "captive," "bound," "anxious," "sad," "depressed," and "fearful"—*these* are words that describe those who do not have a personal relationship with our Lord. For those who know and trust in Him, there is surprising victory over despair, even when we are lacking at weigh-in time.

My friend Chuck Swindoll once provided me with a keen insight on this biblical principle. As I counseled with him regarding my ministry and personal matters, he reminded me to "stay surprised—our God is wonderfully equipped to answer our every need."

Have you ever noticed how the Lord takes delight in surprising us? Life in ministry is filled with surprises. It is usually when we come to the end of ourselves that He steps in and says, "My way, not your way." Christ is at His best when we are at the end of our resources. In our weakness, we say "no way"; in His strength, the Lord says "My way."

We are reminded of this principle in 2 Corinthians 12:9-10, where the Lord informs the apostle Paul, "My grace is sufficient for you, for my power is made perfect in weakness." Paul was weak, but the Lord's strength was more than sufficient to make up for his frailty.

When we say "impossible," God says "it is done." He says, "I know you can't do it. I made you weak so you would trust in Me."

Overcoming Frustration Through Faith

The fisherman's life is not an easy one. There are many times of great frustration. We often need to trust in God for endurance and patience, especially during those times when we suffer through the agony of defeat.

Jesus takes broken, frustrated, confused men and teaches them about Himself and how to become His disciples. In return, He asks only that we give all of ourselves to Him.

My Bible is open to one of my favorite sections of Luke's Gospel where we learn a great lesson from the Lord's disciple-fishermen:

> One day as Jesus was standing by the Lake of Gennesaret, with the people crowding around him and listening to the word of God, he saw at the water's edge two boats, left there by the fishermen, who were washing their nets. He got into one of the boats, the one belonging to Simon, and asked him to put out a little from shore. Then he sat down and taught the people from the boat.
>
> When he had finished speaking, he said to Simon, "Put out into deep water, and let down the nets for a catch."
>
> Simon answered, "Master, we've worked hard all night and haven't caught anything. But because you say so, I will let down the nets."
>
> When they had done so, they caught such a large number of fish that their nets began to break. So they signaled their partners in the other boat to come and help them, and they came and filled both boats so full that they began to sink.
>
> When Simon Peter saw this, he fell at Jesus' knees and said, "Go away from me, Lord; I am a sinful man!" For he and all his companions were astonished at the catch of fish they had taken, and so were James and John, the sons of Zebedee, Simon's partners.
>
> Then Jesus said to Simon, "Don't be afraid; from

now on you will catch men." So they pulled their boats up on shore, left everything and followed Him. (Luke 5:1-11)

In the first few verses of this passage, we find the Capernaum Fishing Company—Peter, Andrew, James, and John—returning from a fishless night on the Sea of Galilee. Today's fishermen can escape the merciless comments of competing colleagues by retreating to a launch ramp. But these disheartened fishermen of old were along the shore-line, out in the open, washing their nets in a freshwater spring area.

Scripture *and* modern-day fishermen on the Sea of Galilee tell us that most of the fishing in this area is done at night. The fish frequent the shallow waters in the late evening and early morning hours. They are also drawn toward light. So, the fish would have been drawn to the oil lamps or small fires on the disciples' boats.

As the multitude followed Jesus and pressed Him to speak, He recognized the discouragement of His disciples along the shore. As Jesus spoke and the crowd grew, Peter and the other disciples listened but were preoccupied with their inability to catch fish and with the chores associated with taking care of their equipment.

Jesus seized the moment and asked to use Peter's boat as a platform from which to continue His message. Our Lord knew that the water would serve as an amplifier for His voice while giving Him some separation from the ever-pressing crowd.

Jesus appreciated Peter's obedience in small things (providing the boat and pushing it offshore). Now it was time to test Peter in the bigger things (packing up the net and moving out to deep water at midday—typically a poor time to fish).

Yet we find Peter not questioning Jesus, but obeying Him. As a fisherman, Peter knew how hopeless it was to "let down his net" at that time. He had his doubts about what he was being told to do. But as an act of obedience, at Christ's word and upon His command, Peter did as he was told.

Christ saw that Peter's heart was open even though he was discouraged, defeated, and embarrassed. He was probably one of the best fishermen in all of Israel and he could not catch a single fish. All those following Christ had their eyes upon Peter and his companions as they made their way out into deeper, more unproductive waters.

I can see the disciples letting down their nets, wondering how a carpenter might use this exercise as a teaching event. Within minutes, their nets were full of fish—so many that their nets began to break. They loaded the fish on board Peter's boat but soon realized that another boat was needed. James and John quickly made their way to the nets in their boat and finished pulling in the record catch.

Simon Peter was so awestruck and shamed at the doubt he displayed in Christ's ability to provide that he "fell down at Jesus' feet, saying, 'Depart from me, for I am a sinful man, O Lord'" (Luke 5:8 NASB).

Again, Jesus, ever so patiently, reminded Peter and the disciples of His challenge and call: "Don't be afraid; from now on *you will catch men*" (Luke 5:10, emphasis added). The counsel to His disciples was that from now on they would be fishers of men. And the men that were "caught" would not be held as trophies but would be released back into the world.

Insights for Living

What can we learn from Peter's experience? I believe we can see at least five principles that will encourage us on those dark days when the sun does not seem to shine upon us—when our livewells are empty and the grandstand is full of critics and scorners.

Be an Obedient Disciple

First, we are called to be obedient disciples. Peter was obedient in responding to the simple request of his Master.

Without hesitation he allowed Jesus to use his boat as a platform for speaking.

I am sure Peter was extremely tired and was probably not even finished cleaning his boat. He could have denied Jesus' request and asked Him to use someone else's boat that hadn't been used for fishing all night. He could have asked Jesus to speak from the hill behind him where He would later preach the Sermon on the Mount.

Peter did neither. He was obedient in the small things. He learned from previous lessons that Jesus blesses obedience.

Peter gave the Lord what he had—an old wooden fishing boat and a little of his time. Little did Peter know that when Jesus saw his faithfulness in this simple request, he would be asked to extend even more effort and faith to eventually receive a bountiful blessing (a boat overflowing with fish!).

The renowned pastor and aspiring fisherman, Charles Stanley, provides us with some insights on the issue of obedience:

> Remember that obedience is doing what God says, when He says, and how He says. To be partially obedient is disobedience. You will never know what your life could have been like if you are not totally obedient. Why risk losing a blessing when you can be sure of winning His trust.[1]

Peter did *what* Jesus said, *when* He said, and *how* He said. You and I are called to do the same.

Some disciples have not been obedient to the Lord in the small things and they wonder why they have not received many blessings in life. When we are called of God to do a task, we should respond as Peter did.

For some it is easier to let the other guy do it. Others use the excuse that there will always be someone more qualified or less busy who can do the task. If God gives *you* the call or vision for a particular assignment, then He expects *you* to tackle it.

Others believe that unless they are the leader or primary person in charge, they are wasting their gifts to do lesser tasks. Again, Peter's obedience gives us some insight into how God works. We are to be obedient in the simplest of duties *no matter what our qualifications*. God will develop you as a leader *if you are first willing to be a servant*.

I found that my ministry became bigger and more powerful when I adopted a "servant's heart." When I humbled myself to accept and complete the task before me—*no matter how small*—then my Lord could trust and bless me with mightier responsibilities.

Fifteen years ago, I believed I should be speaking at the major conference centers. Dr. Jim Dobson was missing out by not putting me on his radio program. And since my vision for ministry was so unique, I believed every church in the country needed to hear my messages.

What I discovered is that God wanted me to be faithful in preaching His message to a group of ten at a men's fellowship in a small church. He directed me to assist other ministries with their programs. Christ helped me to see that I needed to be obedient with His *small* requests. Then He would give me a bigger ministry. And, indeed, He has!

When we learn to serve others without regard to self, then God can use our humble spirit to do mightier works. It has been said, "At the foot of the cross we never stand higher than the feet of Jesus." We need to demonstrate Christ's servant heart by "washing the feet" of (or *serving*) the people He has called us to lead (John 13:5).

Jesus called disciples who would ultimately be willing to rely upon Him instead of relying on their foolish self-competency. Jesus seeks men who have a passion for life and a commitment to obedience.

As others see our obedience and faith, they become like-minded. Our actions, our servant's heart, and our diligence speak volumes to them of our deep love and commitment to serve.

Discipleship Requires Teamwork

Our individual efforts alone will not be as effective as working with others. Teamwork is a key to effective ministry.

Jesus involved many people in His work—even in His miracle of blessing Peter with abundant fish. Jesus apparently involved a number of village fishermen-disciples in this miracle. Due to the size of the boat (about 8 feet by 27 feet) and the netting strategies required to use a trammel net, some men were required to row the boat, some to drop the nets, and some to pull up fish.[2]

The disciples were team players. Net fishing requires cooperation and trust. Unlike modern tournament fishing, which is usually one-on-one, these Galileans could not handle their responsibilities alone. Jesus knew that selfless teamwork was required to be a good fisherman. He also knew of its importance to effective ministry.

It is still true today. Christ desires a company of team players who have a servant's heart—a desire to put others above self. He calls men to humble themselves and to wash the feet of the downtrodden, the poor, the disabled, the weak, and the unlovable. He seeks men willing to place into service their gifts, talents, and their most prized possessions.

Look to the Familiar to Teach the Incredible

To help the disciples understand and accept Him, Jesus came to their turf. He went into the marketplace of their lives. He used the *familiar* to teach them the *incredible*. The sea, an old wooden boat, their fishing skills, worn-out equipment, and the fishery at the Sea of Galilee were all performers in the play that was presented to the disciples.

Jesus did not take them to unfamiliar turf and threaten them with hell and damnation. He did not preach over their heads to humble them into submission. Christ could have revealed His power and authority by drying up the lake and walking out and collecting the fish in a basket. But He did not do that.

Our Lord was gentle and patient as He used the *familiar*

to help teach a lesson of obedience to the disciples. By using such a "user-friendly environment," He was able to relate to them in a special way.

When we begin to disciple unbelievers, we look for ways to connect with them. They have a comfort zone with familiar surroundings. If we are to be most effective, we must utilize those places and tools that do not threaten or present an uncomfortable setting.

A key to the success of Let's Go Fishing Ministries is that we try to present our programs in the comfortable outdoor environment. This unstructured atmosphere allows people to focus in on our words and actions instead of being distracted by the often threatening environment of a church.

Do not misunderstand what I'm saying. I strongly believe in and support the local church. Over half our programs are conducted in the church and are presented to audiences who are believers. However, my experience in doing over 300 conference programs and sports shows is that most unsaved people initially feel more comfortable in an environment they know and understand.

Maybe that comfortable environment is a Let's Go Fishing program, or a fishing trip to the local lake, or another community-type event that eliminates barriers. Perhaps it is something as simple as inviting your neighbor to a barbecue cookout in your backyard.

God simply wants us to be obedient in using the *familiar*, so that He can do the *miraculous*. He will provide the miracles of changed lives if we are faithful in relating to people in their comfort zones.

Disciples Are Flexible

A disciple is flexible and is not afraid to take risks. Peter remained flexible in his attitude and spirit. Despite his knowledge and understanding of fishing, he remained open to new ideas and approaches. He was not arrogant or prideful, but was willing to adapt and explore.

When Jesus asked Peter to go out into deep water, it presented a risk to Peter and his companions. They knew how unforgiving the sea could be in the middle of the day when the wind was at its worst. They knew the security of the shoreline would be a distant memory once they went to the deeper water. There was also the risk of not catching any fish and being further humiliated.

Again, though, we see Peter's trust and obedience as he followed the Master's command: "Because you say so, I will let down the nets" (Luke 5:5). Peter knew from experience that Jesus' command carried with it assurances of success and blessing.

A disciple that truly understands and experiences the freedom that grace offers will become more flexible in his attitudes and allow himself to take more risk. He will trust God to move him from the *safety of the seen* to the *wonder of the unseen*.

Anyone can cast a net into the shallow water of life that is characterized by the known and the friendly. We need not leave the comfort and security of the shoreline to experience that. We can just write a check to a missions program and feel we have responded.

It takes some risk and a lot of trust, however, to venture into the unknown and sometimes unfriendly deep waters of life. Once we have accepted a call to visit the mission field or participate in a church outreach activity, only then are we risking and stretching our faith.

Obeying God may sometimes involve doing things to receive the blessing that may seem unreasonable. When I left 20 years of public service and a very secure job to go into ministry, it was one of those tests. *What risk is God asking you to take for Him?*

Obedience Brings Blessing

Peter and the other disciples could discern the deity of Christ in the events that transpired around them. One thing *we* learn from the experiences of the disciples is that Jesus sometimes conceals His power until we follow His leading. It was only when Peter followed his Master's command and risked going into the deep water that the blessing could be experienced.

Why take a risk? *Because God will change your life!*

An obedient disciple will see God's power demonstrated through his life. Obeying God never proves to be a disappointment. Jesus can turn our "nothing" into a "something."

Jesus reveals His purpose to those who are willing to relinquish their security. When we follow Him, we will fully experience the breaking of our nets and the filling of our boats. *The potential is incredible.*

And if we want to be effective disciplers *of others*, we must take personal responsibility to show the way to those we are training. While we are not perfect like our Lord, we must take the faith we have and encourage those who are just beginning to cast out their nets. They need to know we can expect a miracle and be blessed with full nets once we put our trust in Him who is able.

Personal Growth

- What have you learned in this chapter that can help you better face discouragement in your life?

- What does it mean to be an obedient disciple?

- How are you working with others to answer the challenge put forth in Matthew 28:19?

Chapter Ten

Reflection
"When the Tournament Is Over"

As I packed up my Suburban and headed down the road, my thoughts focused on the events of the past three days. I was frustrated with myself for the poor strategy decisions I made in fishing the prestigious Jimmy Rogers Invitational Bass Tournament. The pattern that had given me second place the day before changed Saturday evening with a passing cold front. Saturday's keeper fish moved to shallow water and left behind dozens of smaller fish that would continue to tease me all day long.

Each cast produced a bite and often an undersized fish. The temptation to throw them back in and find the "big ones" was more than I could stand. As the day wore on, my position as the "person most likely to win" became but a mere fantasy. I had blown the biggest tournament in the west.

My feelings of failure and frustration were no better the following Monday morning. I had to face the daily grind called "work," and the "Monday Morning Blues" followed me throughout the day. My negative attitude caused me to view the circumstances of the day with disdain and sarcasm.

I needed a change of heart and a fresh perspective. It was definitely time to talk with God about things.

I reminded myself that with the help of the Holy Spirit, I had the power to accept my failures and move on with life. The combination of repentant prayer and a little time led to a change in my attitude.

Looking beyond the circumstances of the weekend, I was able to focus on the tangible blessings that surround me. I have a loving wife, two wonderful sons, a good job, several caring Christian friends, and, most of all, a Savior who cares. What more could a guy ask for? Knowing that my Savior listens with compassion provided me with the comfort I needed.

The Monday Morning Blues

Even the most committed disciple can experience the Monday Morning Blues—those times when life seems to press you to the mat and your self-esteem is in desperate need of a resurrection. The situation immediately following Christ's crucifixion was one such time for the first-century disciples.

Much has been written about the crucifixion of Christ and His resurrection from the dead. But relatively little attention has been given to the 11 disciples who were left to sort out their lives in light of their "call to ministry." When Christ was taken for trial and His fate became known to the disciples, we see these cowardly, confused men scatter throughout the countryside. Their disappointment and discouragement must have seemed overwhelming.

In John 21 we catch a glimpse into the mindset of the disciples. Though the risen Christ had already appeared to them twice (Luke 24:16-32; John 20:19-29), the disciples continued to feel the pain associated with losing their good friend and teacher. The reunion had been all too brief and incomplete. Their hearts longed for comfort and love as they contemplated the future.

Without their Master and the filling of the Holy Spirit,

they were left to their own inadequate devices and power. The disciples were no different from any other broken-hearted individual. Understandably, they returned to the people, places, and routines that would bring them comfort and security. They returned to the one thing they knew they could do—*fishing*.

As we pick up the story in John 21, we see seven of the fishermen-disciples night-fishing on the Sea of Tiberias. But even that became a challenge. They toiled all night long, and there was failure there, too.

Things were looking bad for the disciples. Life was tough. As we read in John 21:2-3,

> Simon Peter, Thomas (called Didymus), Nathanael from Cana in Galilee, the sons of Zebedee, and two other disciples were together. "I'm going out to fish," Simon Peter told them, and they said, "We'll go with you." So they went out and got into the boat, *but that night they caught nothing.* (emphasis added)

The Risen Christ Intervenes

Perhaps it had been some time since the Savior last revealed Himself to the disciples. Maybe their memories of past miracles and teachings were clouded by their immediate physical needs for food and rest. Whatever the reason, the disciples were not expecting their Master to present Himself on this inauspicious occasion.

The long cold night was coming to an end and a new day was dawning. As the sky brightened in the east, there appeared a shadow along the shoreline. A voice came from the direction of the shadow, asking the disciples, "Friends, haven't you any fish?"

"No," they answered (John 21:5).

Nothing is more humbling to a fisherman than to be asked that probing question. When your creel is empty, there will almost always be someone asking you to report on the fruits of your labor. Then there are days when your basket is full, but you can't find anyone to hear your bragging tales. It does not seem fair. Yet through it all, God has a way of helping us see things in perspective.

This brings to mind a story I often tell when introducing a famous fisherman like Jimmy Houston. It seems that a good friend of Jimmy's died and went to heaven. This young guy could not understand why he would be called home at such a young age.

He approached St. Peter and asked him why he was called home. St. Peter suggested that he go over to the "Big Fishing Room in the Sky" and ask the attendant at the door.

The young fisherman made his way over to the room and asked the attendant, "Why did I get called home so soon?"

The attendant replied that his "clock had stopped. And when your clock stops you are called home to glory."

As they slowly walked through the large room filled with clocks, the attendant went on to explain that every fisherman has a clock. As Jimmy's young friend looked around at all the clocks, he noticed a minute hand that moved ahead. He asked the door attendant, "What does it mean when the minute hand moves forward?"

The attendant explained, "That means the fisherman just caught a fish."

The fisherman looked around at all the clocks with individual names beneath them and asked, "What does it mean when the minute hand moves backward?"

"That means a fisherman just told an untruth or exaggeration," the attendant responded.

Our young fisherman continued to look all around when he asked one more question: "Well, where is Jimmy Houston's clock?"

The attendant smiled and pointed to the corner of the room and said, "It's over in the corner. We use it as a fan!"

Fishermen are just that way. When we are successful, we want everyone to know it. When we fail, we embellish the stories and make excuses.

Fortunately, the first-century fishermen had the greatest

fisherman of all—the Lord Jesus—on their side. Because Jesus did not want His distraught fishermen friends to be frustrated any further, He interceded.

Overflowing Nets—Abundant Blessings

Just as He had done earlier when the disciples failed to catch any fish (Luke 5), Jesus yet again sought to connect with His disciples in the activity and work they best understood. His goal was that this miracle would impress upon them His abiding love and care—as well as His omniscience and omnipotence—even more.

Jesus said, "Throw your net on the right side of the boat and you will find some." When the disciples did as they were instructed, "they were unable to haul the net in because of the large number of fish" (John 21:6).

Can you imagine what these professional fishermen must have been thinking? I am sure they wondered, "Who is this guy that he can instruct us on how and where to fish?" I can hear them saying, "Well, we have tried everything else. Let's give this a try." With their weary, tired bodies, they threw out just one more cast.

Suddenly there were fish—so many that the fishermen could not haul them into the boat. Then John, "the apostle Christ loved," recognized the miracle taking place as well as the miracle-maker who had called out to them. *It was Jesus.* Jesus had returned to the very shores from whence He first called them (Matthew 4:19).

> Then the disciple whom Jesus loved [John] said to Peter, "It is the Lord!" As soon as Simon Peter heard him say, "It is the Lord," he wrapped his outer garment around him (for he had taken it off) and jumped into the water. (John 21:7)

The trammel or gill net they were using occasionally required one of the fishermen to disrobe and dive into the lake to untangle the bottom before it could be hauled in. Peter was therefore without clothes.

Now, the Jews regarded a greeting as a religious act that could be done *only* when one was clothed. Therefore, Peter, in wrapping his outer garment around himself, prepared to greet the Master—his King.

The oarsmen were not making enough progress toward shore for Peter, who was so filled with joy and excitement that he could not contain himself. So he jumped in and swam the 100 yards—clothes and all—in what I am sure was record time. "The other disciples followed in the boat, towing the net full of fish, for they were not far from shore" (John 21:8). The Scriptures tell us,

> When they landed, they saw a fire of burning coals there with fish on it, and some bread. Jesus said to them, "Bring some of the fish you have just caught." Simon Peter climbed aboard and dragged the net ashore. It was full of large fish, 153, but even with so many the net was not torn. Jesus said to them, "Come and have breakfast." None of the disciples dared ask him, "Who are you?" They knew it was the Lord. (John 21:9-12)

Object Lessons from the Sea of Galilee

The disciples' catch of fish was a result of the combined efforts of Christ's miracle and their backbreaking netting strategies. Perhaps this is an illustration of how God's gift of the Holy Spirit and man's talents can be combined to harvest "fish" (human beings) for His kingdom. The full nets may have represented the success of the disciples' future ministry. They no doubt recognized that the spiritual drought in their own lives was over and it was now time to begin the harvest of lost souls.

Unlike the earlier miracle in which their nets broke because of so many fish (Luke 5), their nets *did not* break on *this* trip, and the fish were all "keepers"—quality fish. The net "was full of large fish, 153, but even with so many the net was not torn" (John 21:8-9).

Despite the load of fish, the net held together and no fish were lost. This miracle illustrates the protection and security a believer has with his Lord. Every "fish" (Christian) is a precious soul. Christ continually abides with us, and once "fish" are caught (saved), they are *always* saved.

After blessing the food, the disciples enjoyed a wonderful meal with their Savior. As they were finishing their food, the Master once again challenged their faith, reminding them of His promises and provisions.

The disciples stared into Christ's face, silently reflecting on all He had said and the many times they had shared meals around the campfire. I am sure a contemplative mood reigned during the meal. Their observations of the Master provided additional assurance and confirmation that Jesus truly is God.

Peter's Restoration

At this time Jesus gave Peter—the apostle who had denied Him three times—a chance to redeem himself. We read in Scripture,

> Jesus said to Simon Peter, "Simon son of John, do you truly love me more than these?" "Yes, Lord," he said, "you know that I love you." Jesus said, "Feed my lambs." (John 21:15)

Jesus called on Peter to affirm his love and dedication. Did he love the Lord more than his fishing friends? Did he love the Lord more than fishing itself? *Peter said yes.*

So our loving Savior encouraged Peter to take care of the young sheep—*lambs*. It was important to Christ that Peter's haughty spirit be challenged and that he understood the importance of taking care of the tender of heart—the spiritually immature disciples.

To drive home the point even more, Christ asked the same question again, but with a little different slant. We read,

> Again Jesus said, "Simon son of John, do you truly love me?" He answered, "Yes, Lord, you know that I love you." Jesus said, "Take care of my sheep." (John 21:16)

Peter's previous action of denying Christ three times required a renewal of Christ's call on Peter's life and a reestablishment of Peter's position. Toward this end Christ asked Peter to "feed" or "keep" His sheep. He was asking Peter to tend and shepherd His flock.

This call to a pastoral vocation was a pronouncement of trust and recommitment. Christ recognized Peter's leadership qualities and wanted to direct his talent.

But Christ was not yet through with Peter. He wanted to remind him to count the cost of discipleship by testing the sincerity of his love and commitment.

The third time Christ asked the question brought to Peter's mind the recollection of his threefold denial of Christ. Peter's heart was engulfed in sadness and shame. Peter clearly saw his responsibility to be a committed disciple to the point of death. Scripture tells us,

> The third time he said to him, "Simon son of John, do you love me?" Peter was hurt because Jesus asked him the third time, "Do you love me?" He said, "Lord, you know all things; you know that I love you." Jesus said, "Feed my sheep." (John 21:17)

Peter not only stated his deepest love for the Lord but recognized Christ's infinite knowledge and grasp of his personal situation. Christ saw that Peter's love involved his will and total personality. He could see that Peter was now ready to be molded and shaped for ministry. Peter now accepted Jesus as both Savior *and* Lord of his life.

Then for the last time Christ issued the call to Peter and the other disciples: "Follow me!" (John 21:19). Their lives would never be the same. They would all go on to testify of

His kingdom and power. Peter would go on to be the "rock" Christ identified in John 1:42.

Peter was now prepared to help others endure the persecutions and sufferings that would be their fate as Christians. He would encourage believers to set their minds on the glory to come. With love and humility, he began to model courage and grace.

Lessons to Live By

All of us can learn some lessons from the experiences of the disciples that Monday morning after the Resurrection. Much like our first-century brothers and sisters, we all experience times of great frustration and disappointment. Part of living in an imperfect world is that we can expect discouraging events in our lives.

Of course, in most cases it is not the situation itself that creates despair *but how we choose to react to it*. God desires that we react or respond to the circumstances of life with faith. Those who walk in faith do not succumb to despair.

I believe we can draw four principles of encouragement from our fishing friends of old. Consider how they apply to *your* life.

God Meets Us at Our Greatest Point of Need

The disciples were already frustrated, disappointed, and discouraged as they launched their boat for an evening's fishing. By morning they were even more disappointed because of their failure to catch fish. Having just returned from Jerusalem where they had been ministering, they probably did not have much in the way of a food supply. They were afraid, confused, tired, and hungry.

When things seemed at their worst, Jesus was there to meet and greet the disciples with food and fellowship. After He met their physical needs, He encouraged them emotionally and spiritually by taking time to be with them. With all the things Christ *could* have done prior to His ascension into heaven, He took time to prepare a barbecue cookout for some hurting friends.

As we disciple others, we need to be sensitive to their basic needs. We must not only feed them with the Word of God, we must also deal with the hurts they have. Through the lifestyle evangelism ministry God has given me, we have been able to provide tangible encouragement and support to individuals with real needs.

If a person has a need to learn how to fish, *then we provide instruction.* If a single parent mom needs some financial assistance so she can attend one of our parenting conferences, *then we get involved.* If an estranged father and son need someone to come beside them and provide relational materials and counseling that will assist them in building a strong relationship, *then we respond.* That is what ministry is all about.

Addressing perceived needs in others requires sensitivity and time. *Christ took the time.* By taking time to be with His disciples, He showed compassion and love. In today's fast-paced world, disciples spell the word *love* T-I-M-E.

When we take time to relate to people and understand their ambitions, dreams, desires, and needs, we are able to better relate and apply God's Word. We earn the right to be heard about the things of the Lord.

Jesus Understands Monday Morning Blues

At the cross, Jesus experienced the ultimate rejection. Fellowship with the Father was broken. His disciples and friends abandoned Him. He felt the pain and anguish of sinful humankind. With the despair of a broken heart, He cried out from that cross, "My God, my God, Why hast thou forsaken me?" (Matthew 27:46 KJV). Jesus understands what it means to hurt.

Christ is aware of all the hurts and fears that create despair *within our* hearts. He knows our pain and loss as we pick ourselves up after defeat. It is because He has sensitivity to our hopelessness that He can be our divine comforter and companion (Hebrews 4:15).

The psalmist reminds us, "Cast your burden upon the

LORD, and He will sustain you; He will never allow the right-eous to be shaken" (Psalm 55:22 NASB).

Jesus Is Still the Miracle-Worker

As Jesus performed miracles in the presence of His disci-ples, they perceived His deity and His concern for humankind. If we are sensitive to His spirit, *we too* will see His miracles—the miracle of a newborn baby, the miracles of nature, those miracles of life that *only you* have seen, and most of all, the miracle of His saving grace to all of us sin-ners.

I am reminded of a story about two fishermen whose out-board motor quit as they were trying to make their way back to the shore. As they struggled against the approaching storm, they spotted another boat, but they never called out for help.

A short time later, a helicopter passed overhead. But again, they never indicated their emergency.

As their boat flipped over, two life jackets floated to the top. But the unobservant fishermen never grabbed hold of them.

When they reached heaven, they asked, "God why didn't you help us? Couldn't you see that we needed a miracle?"

God simply smiled and said, "I sent a boat, a helicopter, and gave you two life jackets, but you didn't accept any of them."

Yes, Jesus still performs miracles. Are you casting your net of faith daily expecting a miracle? *I stay surprised.* Despite all the technology and knowledge surrounding us, I still look upward awaiting God's next miracle in my life and the lives of those I love. Keep an expectant heart and an open mind about how God can rescue you with His special blessings.

Jesus Issues a Progressive Call—"Follow Me!"

In John 1:39 we find Christ approaching His disciples and asking them to follow Him. He said, "Come, and you will see." The call in Matthew 4:18-19 had a similar meaning to the disciples.

The disciples first had a period of time to learn from the Master—to watch and work with Him. While they believed in Him as Savior, they were not yet ready to unreservedly submit to Him as absolute Lord of their lives. The "come and see" period was a time when they could test their thinking and refine the depth of their commitment.

Today Jesus asks us to consider the same call. He does not want us fishing for men until we have first considered and accepted Him as our Savior *and* Lord. He wants us to study His life so that we can truly follow His ways.

We witness another call to discipleship in Luke 5. Jesus called the disciples to consider changing their vocation from *fishing for fish* to *fishing for men*. This call occurred after the disciples had already spent some time with the Master. Jesus had lived with Peter and his family in Capernaum for several months. The disciples had heard His messages, witnessed His miracles, and studied His teachings. Their hearts had been transformed and relationships were firmly established.

As we mature in our faith and become more aware of the Holy Spirit's influence in our lives, we (like Jesus' disciples) want to become more like the Master. The personal habits and attitudes that are not Christ-like become out of place in our daily walk. As the Holy Spirit works conviction in our hearts, our desire is to give up those things unbecoming to a child of the King. As the Holy Spirit influenced the lives of the disciples, so He influences our lives as well.

In John 21:19 we see Christ's final call to His disciples. After sharing with Peter a prediction on how he would die a martyr's death, Jesus called His disciples and simply said, "Follow me."

Peter in this verse was being asked to stretch his faith one more time. Was he willing to forsake everything until death for Jesus? Just how deep would his commitment be to serving the God of the universe?

Bible expositors Robert Jamieson, A. R. Fausset, and David Brown summarize this verse in a wonderful way:

By thus connecting this prediction [of Peter's death] with the invitation to follow Him, the Evangelist would indicate the deeper sense in which the call was understood, not merely to go along with Jesus at that moment, but to come after Him, take up His cross. [1]

Go Make Disciples

Jesus told His disciples,

All authority has been given to me in heaven and on earth. Go therefore and make disciples of all nations, baptizing them in the name of the Father and the Son and the Holy Spirit, teaching them to observe all that I commanded you; and lo, I am with you always, even to the end to the age. (Matthew 28:19-20)

The progression of the call to follow Jesus was now complete. For the first time, the disciples could understand and accept that they were responsible to make *new* disciples—to establish Christ's church.

They would not be alone in this task. Jesus promised the disciples they would receive new power from the Holy Spirit (John 14–16). This would equip them for the work of ministry.

At Pentecost, the disciples received the promised gift of the Holy Spirit which enabled them to fulfill their call (Acts 2). They were now able to approach discipleship with a whole new commitment and zeal.

When we accept Jesus as Savior and Lord, the Holy Spirit can provide us the same power as those first-century disciples. We are a new creation in Christ Jesus (2 Corinthians 5:17). Our old self gives way to our new personality.

Like the disciples, we have a new confidence. Listen to what some first-century people said about the spirit-filled disciples: "Now as they observed the confidence of Peter and John, and understood that they were uneducated and untrained men, they were marveling, and began to recognize them as having been with Jesus" (Acts 4:13). We can have this same confidence as we walk in the Spirit (Galatians 5:16).

Are you rigged and ready to go fishing? Is your spiritual life in order? Have you progressed in your discipleship so that you yourself are involved in the process, or are you still sitting on the bank watching others fish and rooting them along without any personal involvement?

Accept Jesus as your Lord and open your life to being a proactive disciple of the King. God may not be leading you into full-time ministry, and that is fine. You have plenty of ministry opportunities right where you are—at work, at home, and within your community.

Disciple, take up your cross and follow Him.

Personal Growth

- Read John 1, Matthew 4, Luke 5, and John 21. Analyze the progressive nature of the discipleship call.

- How would you have responded if you were on the shoreline barbecue with Jesus as described in John 21?

- How much time are you giving to the truly important issues of life?

Learning to Fish
"The Instruction Manual"

As the Executive Director of the Fellowship of Christian Anglers Society (FOCAS), my responsibilities include providing advice and counsel to other organizations and businesses associated with fishing. Such was my pleasure in contributing ideas to some folks in Chattanooga, Tennessee, who were about to build one of the largest aquarium projects in the world.

This aquarium would be utterly unique not only because of its design but because of its emphasis on teaching people about fishing and some basic principles of ecology. Toward this end, Al Lindner and I joined forces to develop a fishing curriculum that could be used with this project and the associated National Fishing Center Project.

The In-Fisherman Communications Network is a world-class organization that utilizes a variety of teaching systems and media to communicate its message. Through television, radio, videotapes, books, magazines, and newsletters, this organization has carefully crafted instructional materials that help motivate anglers in their quest to become better fishermen.

While teaching my "Fundamentals of Fishing" college classes in the late 1960s and early 1970s, I had the opportunity to field-test In-Fisherman's materials along with the assorted programs I had developed. Through these classes, sports show appearances, and involvement with Gary White's Bass Fishing Institutes, I have had the privilege of coaching some two million people on the finer points of fishing.

Al and I agree that most successful fishermen succeed precisely because they've been able to skillfully apply those basic principles received through study and observation. When aspiring anglers take the time to record specific teachings that can assist them with their favorite pursuit, they tend to remember and apply the correct strategy at the appropriate time.

Most of us find it necessary to develop some kind of an "Instruction Manual" or journal that helps us to remember the important points and applications. Contained within the pages of my personal "Fishing Instruction Manual" is the In-Fisherman formula for fishing success. I'm often asked, "How can I learn to fish?" The answer is as simple as learning a little formula, and studying each factor in the formula to better understand how to apply specific abilities and skills.

I realize that some people reading this book may wish to take up this crazy sport. In the following paragraphs, I will provide a brief explanation of the basic theory for being a successful fisherman before sharing the biblical application.

F + L + P = Fishing Success

Learning to fish can be broken down into a simple recipe that will help eliminate those "empty creel days." This formula can be used for either freshwater or saltwater species. The formula was used by our first-century fishermen and is used by tournament pros today.

F — Fish Factor

Before you bait a hook, you better understand the nature of the fish you're attempting to catch. Each species of fish has its own peculiar habits and behavior. Each species responds differently to its environment and to the offerings of a fisherman. Responses to your efforts largely hinge on the particular fish's sense of smell, taste, sight, touch, and hearing.

The individual anatomy of the fish provides a clue as to its limitations and abilities. For example, barracuda and salmon, with their sleek bodies were designed by God to be swift in movement with enormous endurance. The catfish, in contrast, has a flat, wide body that is not conducive to speed but is suited for hugging the bottom while looking for food.

Similarly, sturgeons and sharks have a great sense of smell because of how God created their olfactory glands (smelling organ). The bluegill, in contrast, has a less developed olfactory system, thereby limiting its reliance on smell as a way to survive.

Moreover, each species of fish has its own preferred temperature and oxygen range, food source (forage), and seasonal reproduction process. The more we understand about the "Fish Factor," the better judgments we will make about bait selection and areas to fish.

L — Location Factor

As any good fisherman (or real-estate agent) can tell you, there are three fundamentally important things one must always remember—*location, location, location*. Knowing where to look for those sought-after "honey holes" where schools of fish congregate is a pivotal key to fishing success.

Certain fish, such as a black bass, crappie, or bluegill, typically hang out around warm water near brush piles, logs, piers, pilings, tules, rocks, and grassbeds. Those of us in the fishing industry call this stuff "structure."

In a lake setting, fish such as trout, salmon, and stripers typically cruise about in those open water areas that are well oxygenated with cooler temperatures. Knowing whether the creature is an "open water feeder" or a "close to structure" fish is important in seeking out the proper area in which to make that perfect cast.

Once again, temperature, oxygen, light penetration,

topography, and seasons play an important role in understanding the preferences of a fish on a given day. Even the barometric pressure can have a dynamic effect on the locational patterns of fish.

P — Presentation Factor

Presentation is where "the rubber meets the road." Tackle selection, casting, lure placement, proper use of electronics, and boat placement are all part of the process.

Proper presentation requires constant study, investigation, and practice. If a person understands the first two of these factors and fails to *apply* his knowledge correctly, he will fail to become a good fisherman.

These factors represent the basic building blocks needed to be an effective angler. Patience, perseverance, and concentration cannot be applied if you do not first build the proper foundation.

Similarly, Jesus recognized the importance of building strength and character into His disciples. He asked that each disciple commit totally and wholeheartedly to the principles that would form the superstructure for true discipleship.

Sending Out Apostles

Jesus knew His disciples well. He had seen them study their fishing trade and apply selected strategies to various situations. Now it was time to transfer those teaching techniques to something far more important than a load of fish. *It was time to go fishing for souls.*

It was critically important that Jesus' instructions for "fishing" be understood after He departed. It was through the inspiration of the Holy Spirit that Matthew in his Gospel recorded his Master's words to produce what we might call Jesus' "Instruction Manual of Discipleship."

In Matthew 9:9, Matthew, the final disciple, is selected. By now most of the disciples had been with Christ for some time, witnessing His many miracles and listening to His teaching. As the ultimate instructor, Jesus imparted knowledge that would be used to change the world. His approach was systematic and direct. His building blocks for ministry were clearly set forth as an "Instruction Manual of Discipleship."

The Kingship of Christ

Matthew's Gospel affirms the kingship of Christ. Implied in his affirmation is a call for people everywhere to submit to that kingship. In Matthew 10:2 we meet the 12 men who had openly proclaimed, "Christ is our King." They had sacrificed everything to be His disciples. They gave up their careers and their lifestyles to submit to His authority.

Throughout the first 23 verses of Matthew 10 we find Jesus directing His disciples and giving them "power and authority" for ministry. He instructs them on their immediate mission with respect to where they should stay and what they should do. He warns them that they, like all who would work in the Lord's name, will be persecuted and will come to understand the importance of sacrifice.

Perhaps for that reason, or maybe for the purpose of accountability, Jesus sends them out in pairs. He directs them to seek out the lost while at the same time warning them of the persecution they will face.

Instruction Manual for Discipleship
(Matthew 10:24-42)

In Matthew 10:24-42 Jesus gives His disciples six principles or building blocks to be recorded in their "Instruction Manuals" so they will be properly equipped to meet the challenges before them. While some of His instruction is given explicitly to the 12 disciples, we see that in verse 23 Jesus talks to *future* disciples by suggesting we should work until "the Son of Man comes." His clear word on discipleship was directed to *anyone* calling himself or herself a believer. There is no limitation as to date or relevancy.

1. Be Like Me (Matthew 10:24)

We are called to be like Jesus. "A student is not above his

teacher, nor a servant above his master. It is enough for the student to be like his teacher, and the servant like his master" (Matthew 10:24). That is the bedrock of discipleship. We are to be like our teacher, our master, our Lord, our King. Remember, a disciple is "a leader-in-training—*a learner.*" And we are to have *His* values and priorities.

You might be thinking that this seems to be a recurring theme in Scripture. You would be right. The discussion of discipleship is found throughout Christ's teaching because He desires people to count the cost of following Him. It is fundamental to our faith.

Jesus is perpetually involved in perfecting the saints for the work of ministry—and He uses us in the process. You and I as disciples are to make *other* disciples who can, in turn, reproduce themselves. Discipleship is apprenticeship. It is the process of sharing, encouraging, modeling, teaching, listening, and serving.

All the various aspects of Christ's ministry were directed to maturing His disciples for service. If we are true believers, we should be maturing in *our* faith while encouraging others to mature in *their* faith.

In Matthew 10:24, Christ again reminds His disciples that they must be doers of the Word, not just hearers. Remember, more people will come to Christ by your *modeling* than by your *words.* As my good friend Tim Hansel often says, "We don't need to speak the message; *we are* the message." We are to mimic Him in every way.

A primary ministry of the Holy Spirit is to help us *to be,* not merely *to do.* Scripture tells us, "You will receive power when the Holy Spirit comes on you; and you will *be* my witnesses in Jerusalem, and in all Judea and Samaria, and to th ends of the earth" (Acts 1:8, emphasis added).

Are you more worried about *doing* than *being*? Do your efforts sometimes seem fruitless? Maybe you are more concerned about the *look* of ministry than its *function.*

The Great Commission is often misinterpreted with an emphasis placed upon *the doing.* The primary focus of this commission is upon *making disciples*, not "going," "baptizing," or "teaching." These things are merely the by-products of our discipling efforts.

Ken Carpenter, editor of *Spirit of Revival* magazine, states it this way:

> Discipleship is a process. God's desire is to etch into our lives the imprint of His son, Jesus. He is responsible for the construction process of making us like Christ. But He needs yielded, available individuals willing to be shaped, molded, and carved by His hands.[1]

I think many of us spend too much time wondering what we can do for Jesus rather than what He can do through our yielded lives. Jesus constantly reminds us that our daily walk is our testimony.

Luke 6:40 provides further encouragement to this point: "A student is not above his teacher, but everyone who is fully trained *will be like his teacher*" (emphasis added) The spiritual barometer against which we must continually measure ourselves is encapsulated in the statement, "You say you follow Christ; then show me your Christlikeness."

When I focus upon the character of God and the teachings of Christ, *that* is when I mature in my faith. It really is not important what I think of myself, or what others might think, or how I believe others may see me. What *is* important to understand is how God sees me and how I can better emulate Him in my daily walk.

2. Do Not Be Afraid of the World (Matthew 10:25-31)

Three times in the next seven verses Jesus instructs His disciples to not be afraid:

> So *do not be afraid* of them. There is nothing concealed that will not be disclosed, or hidden that will not be made known. What I tell you in the dark, speak in the daylight; what is whispered in your ear,

proclaim from the roofs. *Do not be afraid* of those who kill the body but cannot kill the soul. Rather, be afraid of the One who can destroy both soul and body in hell. Are not two sparrows sold for a penny? Yet not one of them will fall to the ground apart from the will of your Father. And even the very hairs of your head are all numbered. So *don't be afraid*; you are worth more than many sparrows. (Matthew 10:26-31, emphasis added)

Jesus tries to calm the disciples' fears because they had just heard Him describe a series of troubles they would encounter (Matthew 10:16-23). He had informed them:
- You will be sent out as sheep among wolves (verse 16);
- You will be beaten in the synagogues (verse 17);
- You will be brought before kings and governors (verse 18);
- You will be a prisoner brought before trial (verse 19);
- Your own family will put you to death (verse 21);
- You will be hated by many (verse 22); and
- You will be persecuted for your beliefs (verse 23).

The fear of men can strangle the effectiveness of our ministry. If we become mere men-pleasers, then we will give up on the ideals of our faith. There will be the constant temptation to pull back on our testimony and not be confrontive when the situation dictates.

If we are like Christ, we will be treated like Him. The world treated Christ like the Devil (Beelzebub). "If the head of the house has been called Beelzebub, how much more the members of his household!" (Matthew 10:25).

I think many of us are afraid to go into the world because of what others might think of our love for the Lord. Jesus tells us that there will be a day when everything will be made right. God will make the truth known. He will reward and vindicate His own. We need to maintain an eternal perspective. If we are worried about being popular or wise or noble in today's society instead of confronting an evil world, we've lost our eternal perspective.

I remember sitting in Chuck Swindoll's office after a wonderful lunch and great fellowship when he offered some wise counsel from God's Word. I had been lamenting over my failure to please a few board members. So Chuck had me read Galatians 1:10, which states, "Am I now trying to win the approval of men, or of God? Or am I trying to please men? If I were still trying to please men, I would not be a servant of Christ."

Whose praise are you seeking? Remember that the praise of men can be fickle.

We need to proclaim our allegiance to Christ in public "from the roofs" (Matthew 10:27). Without being obnoxious, we should go out into the world, leaving the security of our churches, and proclaim Him to be the King of kings and Lord of lords. We shouldn't alter our message and lifestyle for fear of what other people's reactions might be. The apostle Paul certainly didn't worry about those who threatened to throw him in jail.

Discipleship involves an identification with Christ in His person *and* His rejection. Paul had it figured out: "I want to know Christ and the power of His resurrection and the fellowship of sharing in his sufferings" (Philippians 3:10).

3. Publicly Confess Jesus Is Lord (Matthew 10:32-33)

If you believe Jesus came to die for your sins, if you believe His power is greater than men, if you believe God is a Father who cares for His children, and if you accept His promise of protection and power, then *you will not fear or be ashamed of the Gospel.* Paul's letter to the Romans testifies to this reality: "I am not ashamed of the gospel, because it is the power of God for the salvation of everyone who believes" (Romans 1:16a).

Christ instructs His disciples, "Whoever acknowledges me before men, I will also acknowledge him before my Father in heaven" (Matthew 10:32). We must be willing to agree, affirm, and confess that Jesus is Lord.

If we believe our faith should be kept a secret, we have missed the purpose of discipleship. We need to be genuine in our commitment. We show that authentic commitment by openly proclaiming His presence in our lives. Once again, the apostle Paul helps us to understand this concept when he challenged the early disciples in Rome: "If you confess with your mouth, 'Jesus is Lord,' and believe in your heart that God raised him from the dead, you will be saved" (Romans 10:9).

A true disciple confesses his faith before men. Jesus then affirms His loyalty to us by acknowledging before our heavenly Father that we are His children, washed in the cleansing blood of the Lamb. If we persist in denying our allegiance to Christ, however, then on the day of judgment Jesus will disown us: "But whoever disowns me before men, I will disown him before my Father in heaven" (Matthew 10:33).

We can deny our faith in numerous ways. Our un-Christian actions and attitudes can deny Him. Keeping silent when a testimony is called for can deny Him. Our lack of encouragement to a struggling brother or sister in the Lord can be a point of denial.

If we sense a conviction of the Holy Spirit when we have failed in this respect, then we need to rethink our response so we won't fail the next time around. To be sure, we have *all* failed in this area. By our nature we all have lapses. If we are repentant and have a sense of brokenness regarding our lapse, then we have the heart of a believer. We can ask God for His grace and move on to live a more Christlike life.

I'm embarrassed to count the number of times God provided the perfect opportunity for me to share my faith, but in my silence I denied Him. Thankfully, as I have matured in the Lord, those times have become fewer and fewer. Are you finding it more comfortable to be a witness?

4. A Commitment to Discipleship May Cause Division (Matthew 10:34-39)

Jesus said, "Do not suppose that I have come to bring peace to the earth. I did not come to bring peace, but a sword" (Matthew 10:34).

This is a paradox to our understanding. While Jesus is the "prince of peace," yet His presence in our lives will split and fracture some of our relationships. There is peace in the one who believes, but to the one who doesn't know Him there will be alienation and rejection. The sword of conviction and dedication will split many relationships.

The extreme example of this division can be seen in the context of a home. Your commitment to Jesus Christ may need to go against the love and harmony of your household. It doesn't have to be that way, but if it comes to holding onto truth and your commitment to discipleship, then one must bear the pain of a divided home. Jesus said,

> For I have come to turn "a man against his father, a daughter against her mother, a daughter-in-law against her mother-in-law—a man's enemies will be the members of his own household." Anyone who loves his father or mother more than me is not worthy of me; anyone who loves his son or daughter more than me is not worthy of me; and anyone who does not take his cross and follow me is not worthy of me. Whoever finds his life will lose it, and whoever loses his life for my sake will find it. (Matthew 10:35-39)

Sometimes rejection can come from friends. I remember well the time when Louise and I decided to make Jesus the Lord of our lives. We worried about the reaction from friends and family. Many of our closest friends and some family members no longer involved us in many of their activities. For a time we felt so alone and dejected. Then we became involved in a local community church and found that God replaced our lost friends many times over with dedicated, loving people who shared our desire to be more Christlike.

Becoming a disciple involves proclaiming the Lordship of Christ in our lives *even* at the cost of losing family and friends.

5. Commitment to the Call (Matthew 10:37-39)

There is one thing even more precious than our relationship with family members—*the love of our own life*. Jesus took His disciples one step further in testing their commitment and dedication: "Anyone who does not take his cross and follow me is not worthy of me. Whoever finds his life will lose it, and whoever loses his life for my sake will find it" (Matthew 10:37-39).

The disciples hadn't at this point heard about Calvary's cross. So, what is the cross Jesus wanted His disciples to take up? The disciples realized He was talking about dying. They were aware of the likelihood that either the Romans or the Jews would ultimately kill them for their passion and beliefs.

A mark of genuineness for a true disciple, then, is the forsaking of self, even to the point of death. Today we do not have Roman soldiers persecuting us, or dens of lions to face. For most people, standing up for personal faith is not a threatening thing. But what if it *were* a life-threatening issue? What if a foreign power suddenly invaded America and all Christians were commanded to leave their faith or die? Read the Book of Revelation, because you may have to one day make that choice. *How will you choose?*

If confronted with this dilemma are we willing to die for Christ's sake? If not, Jesus' teaching is quite clear. If, however, we are willing to pick up our cross and follow Him, we will see the blessings of ministry. The positive eternal rewards of our faith are clear.

There are some things that are "all or nothing." Discipleship is one of those things.

6. Receiving the Rewards of Ministry (Matthew 10:40-42)

Jesus affirmed,

He who receives you receives me, and he who receives me receives the one who sent me. Anyone who receives a prophet because he is a *prophet* will receive a prophet's reward, and anyone who receives a righteous man because he is a *righteous man* will receive a righteous man's reward. And if anyone gives even a cup of cold water to one of these little ones because he is my disciple, I tell you the truth, he will certainly not lose his reward. (Matthew 10:40-42, emphasis added)

As seen in the first five principles, there exists for every disciple the potential for division and persecution. However, there exists an even greater potential that God could use you for expanding His kingdom. If we are striving to be like Him, then when someone receives us *they receive the Lord*.

A disciple's character as manifest in his speaking (as a prophet) and living (as a righteous man) becomes a source of testimony to the world in which we live. Even the small acts of kindness to "the little ones"—people young in the faith— will be rewarded by our Lord.

A disciple is in part a determiner of destiny for those with whom he comes into contact. He is the hook that God can use to fish the ponds of life, periodically catching a soul.

As His disciples we need to evaluate the depth of our commitment in light of His "Instruction Manual." Are we willing to identify with Him without fear, while publicly confessing and submitting to the point of forsaking family or even loosing our own lives? That is what Jesus asked His first-century disciples to do. *This is what He asks of us today.*

Personal Growth

- Did you notice the increasing levels of sacrifice our Lord demanded of His followers in order to be a committed disciple? Are you willing to follow Him wholeheartedly?

- Do you confess Christ with your mouth? Is there a Christlikeness in your actions and attitudes?

- How can you "stand up for your faith"?

Go and Make Disciples
"Friendly Conversion"

Fishermen take as much pride in telling a good story as they do in landing a trophy fish. My friend Bill Reinhart shared a wonderful story with me about his first fish. Consider his words:

"No one ever forgets catching their first fish." This statement may be a whopping generality, but the underlying truth is applicable to virtually all sports enthusiasts, regardless of age or gender.

During the Korean War, my father was called back to active duty in the Marine Corps. Mother was determined to not let this domestic bombshell interfere with our summer vacation plans to see the west. So, right on schedule, we piled into her '49 Chevy convertible, left our eastern Pennsylvania home, and headed for parts unknown.

Our route meandered south and west, and after what seemed like endless rolling plains as we passed through Kansas, we approached a gigantic amphitheater of mountains that appeared much like a stairway to heaven. At the top, the bright sun reflected off the snowy peaks, and low drifting clouds lent to the view the silvery luster of paradise. Below, snuggled comfortably in a hollow against the foothills, was Denver, the legendary gateway city of the wild west.

We took day-trips into the Rockies and were virtually consumed by the beauty. We would follow cool canyon walls cradling swift running streams until we found their secret sources in high Alpine meadows fed by melting snow runoff. One day we discovered a small mountain community within commuting distance of Denver, and it was love at first sight.

Evergreen was in every sense a miniature western frontier town in the mountains. The house my mother leased, while not surrounded by a ranch with standing cattle, had a lake in the front yard. We were told that in the wintertime, folks came from all around to ice-skate, and, of course, there was fishing.

Coming from a Pennsylvania mining town where the creeks had long since been choked with coal slag and grime, there had been no fishing in my hometown since the days of my grandparents. Now I was in a place with this wonderful fishing opportunity, and no one to show me the rudiments of fishing.

After settling in, the first place I went to was the local sporting goods store, which was also the grocery store and post office. I explained my problem to the clerk. He told me that fishing season began that weekend and, given my indication that I had very limited funds, he said he knew exactly what I needed. Amidst all the rods and reels there was a small cabinet with a glass counter where pocketknives and handguns were visible beneath. Reaching into it, he pulled out a small wooden frame upon which was wound a mound of green string. At the end of the line was a small lead weight and a hook. He assured me that this was all I needed. When I asked about a fishing license, he was more evasive, but he indicated that because of my age, he didn't think a license would be necessary.

In preparation for the big day, I dug around in the backyard and found a worm and a millipede, but I settled for the worm because the millipede was in an awful rush to get somewhere. On Saturday morning, I awoke before dawn and could not believe my eyes. This quiet, seemingly private lake was overrun with fishermen, nearly shoulder to shoulder, waiting for the first rays of daylight to emerge. With no time for breakfast, I jumped into my jeans and engineer boots and headed around the lake. There wasn't any room in front of our house, so I went to where the little creek fed into the lake. It was shallow there, so most of the fishermen had waded out in their boots to where the water was deeper.

When the sun came up, there was a whir of spinning reels and whipping of casting rods, and I hadn't even unwound the line from my wooden frame. The worm was in the paper bag with the fishing line, and because the bag got wet, the worm was difficult to locate. Once found, he was put on the hook like the man in the store directed, and, remaining true to his instructions, I swung the line around in a circle like a large key chain and let go. The weight and the worm traveled at a slightly upward angle to the water, and when all eight feet of line played out, it jerked back, and plunked into the muddy water. Some of the fishermen did their best to ignore my effort, although my cast had landed in the water near their feet. They just shook their heads condescendingly and cast their lines 20 to 30 yards out in the lake using their modern equipment.

As I began to pull the line in for another try, it felt like it was snagged on something, so I gave a yank and the water splashed and churned. I never considered what I might do if I got a fish on the hook, so I was taken completely by surprise. The fishermen started yelling all sorts of instructions to me, but all I could do was back up until the fish was out of the water. There, flopping in the sand, was a beautiful 10-inch rainbow trout.

The fishermen who were so disdainful before were now looking on incredulously, probably wondering how much good all their new equipment was doing. One got so mad, it appeared as if he was going to throw his rod out into the lake.

I'm not sure what the moral to the story is, but it seems to me that sometimes we miss opportunities close by, by looking too far.[1]

The Opportunities Next Door

Discipleship is a lot like Bill's experience with the trout. You can find all kinds of people with fancy programs who are up to their chest in church business, but fail to see the obvious. We drive 25 miles across town to listen to a preacher talk about discipleship and evangelism. We then collect significant amounts of money to send missionaries to the far corners of the world so that we can comfortably drive right past our unsaved neighbor's house on the way home.

Discipleship starts with you and me. It begins at home. It is not just for the seminary-trained person or for those who have been "called" to a mission in a foreign land.

You need not be a champion fisherman for God in order to be a "fisher of men." There are no tournament standings for disciples. *All* fishers of men are important to God. And remember, it is most often the carefully presented "short cast" that lands the fish.

Evangelism simply involves spreading the gospel. Lifestyle evangelism is really the process discipleship is made of. Joe Aldrich, president of Multnomah School of the Bible and author of two wonderful books on this subject, has carefully crafted some creative ways to introduce people to Christ.

For most of us evangelism means loving people until they ask us why. It's touching people in ways appropriate to your own giftedness so that Christ becomes the issue. God is not asking you to back an unbeliever into a corner to mash mental machinery. He's not calling you to back up the evangelical dump truck and pull the lever. He is calling you to action.[2]

Discipleship involves sharing the gospel naturally and without reservation. It is a strategic cast that is willing to patiently wait for the right bite.

Our Lord used a number of graphic examples to help His followers understand some basic concepts of discipleship. How does God get the attention of a group of fishermen-disciples? He uses the very implements they daily work with to teach them object lessons. He uses fishing implements to teach fishermen how to *fish for men*.

Understanding Lifestyle Evangelism [3]

Be Available: God Can Use You

Lifestyle evangelism is a process that can be broken down into three separate kinds of activities: *preparation, casting,* and *catching*. Let's take a brief look at each of these.

Preparation

You will recall from our chapter on "Preparation and Presentation" that this is a special time of building bridges of friendship to the unbeliever. It is a time that caring and character are of primary interest to the person who is searching. It is a period of cultivation that prepares the searching person's heart for a deeper relationship.

In this phase you should be centered on prayer, social activities, understanding, and serving. Be forewarned that you will often have to tolerate behavior and attitudes that may be difficult to accept. Remember, the person you are building a friendship-bridge to is *in process* and change takes time.

This understanding attitude is perhaps nowhere better illustrated than in John 4 where Jesus encounters the woman at the well:

> The Pharisees heard that Jesus was gaining and baptizing more disciples than John, although in fact it was not Jesus who baptized, but his disciples. When the Lord learned of this, he left Judea and went back once more to Galilee.
>
> Now he had to go through Samaria. So he came to a town in Samaria called Sychar, near the plot of ground Jacob had given to his son Joseph. Jacob's well was there, and Jesus, tired as he was from the journey, sat down by the well. It was about the sixth hour.
>
> When a Samaritan woman came to draw water, Jesus said to her, "Will you give me a drink?" (His disciples had gone into the town to buy food.)
>
> The Samaritan woman said to him, "You are a Jew and I am a Samaritan woman. How can you ask me for a drink?" (For Jews do not associate with Samaritans.)
>
> Jesus answered her, "If you knew the gift of God and who it is that asks you for a drink, you would

have asked him and he would have given you living water."

"Sir," the woman said, "you have nothing to draw with and the well is deep. Where can you get this living water? Are you greater than our father Jacob, who gave us the well and drank from it himself, as did also his sons and his flocks and herds?"

Jesus answered, "Everyone who drinks this water will be thirsty again, but whoever drinks the water I give him will never thirst. Indeed, the water I give him will become in him a spring of water welling up to eternal life."

The woman said to him, "Sir, give me this water so that I won't get thirsty and have to keep coming here to draw water."

He told her, "Go, call your husband and come back."

"I have no husband," she replied.

Jesus said to her, "You are right when you say you have no husband. The fact is, you have had five husbands, and the man you now have is not your husband. What you have just said is quite true."

"Sir," the woman said, "I can see that you are a prophet. Our fathers worshipped on this mountain, but you Jews claim that the place where we must worship is in Jerusalem."

Jesus declared, "Believe me, woman, a time is coming when you will worship the Father neither on this mountain nor in Jerusalem. You Samaritans worship what you do not know; we worship what we do know, for salvation is from the Jews. Yet a time is coming and has now come when the true worshipers will worship the Father in spirit and truth, for they are the kind of worshipers the Father seeks. God is spirit, and his worshipers must worship in spirit and in truth."

The woman said, "I know that Messiah" (called

Christ) "is coming. When he comes, he will explain everything to us."

Then Jesus declared, "I who speak to you am he." Just then his disciples returned and were surprised to find him talking with a woman. But no one asked, "What do you want?" or "Why are you talking with her?"

Then, leaving her water jar, the woman went back to the town and said to the people, "Come, see a man who told me everything I ever did. Could this be the Christ?" They came out of the town and made their way towards him. . . .

Many of the Samaritans from that town believed in him because of the woman's testimony, "He told me everything I ever did" (John 4:1-30,39).

As Jesus interacted with this woman, He displayed obvious love and concern for her, despite her past. He didn't speak harsh words of condemnation, but instead built a bridge. And the bridge He built to her that day ultimately led to many Samaritans believing in Him. You and I are called to follow Jesus' example in building such bridges.

Casting

During this phase the unbeliever is searching for answers to his questions. Effective and timely communication is of utmost importance. This is a time when the person's heart is open to multiple and repeated conversations about basic biblical truths.

First Peter 3:15 instructs us, "Always be prepared to give an answer to everyone who asks you to give the reason for the hope that you have." There *will* come a time when the person will ask you *why* you believe *what* you believe. *You must be prepared to answer that question.*

During this time you need to plant seeds of truth that require a lot of tender love and care mixed with a great deal of patience. Throughout the process it is critical to exalt our

Lord and Savior Jesus Christ—not just in what you say but in your behavior as well. This prepares the way for the critical activity of "catching."

Catching

The focus now becomes that of leading the person to a response—a response that says "yes" to Jesus Christ and a lifetime of discipleship. Gentle persuasion and encouragement are in order. Also important is introducing the person to some good Christian literature and a healthy church environment. These will help the new believer/disciple grow and mature in his or her new faith.

A more intense form of discipleship is required to help the person bridge the old life into the new creation. Repentance and sanctification (to purify and make holy) will be part of the process. "But we ought always to thank God for you, brothers loved by the Lord, because from the beginning God chose you to be saved through the sanctifying work of the Spirit and through belief in the truth" (2 Thessalonians 2:13).

Our responsibility as disciples is to be available for the leading of the Holy Spirit. If we realize that the Holy Spirit is ultimately in control of things, then the pressure is off. We need not worry if every word we say is perfect for each person we are discipling. We can simply do our best and then leave everything in the hands of the Holy Spirit.

The following illustration entitled "The Process of Evangelism" is taken from the *CBMC-Lifestyle Evangelism Booklet*. Study it and read the related Scripture verses for understanding and clarification. As you begin to work the process of evangelism in your own life, you will become a more effective Christian *and* disciple.

THE PROCESS

Phase One
PREPARATION
(CULTIVATING)

the **ELEMENTS**	LAKE OR WATER— Human Hearts
the **EXPLANATION**	Speaks to the heart through relationship. Focus is on caring.
the **EMPHASIS**	Presence of the believer builds a friendship bridge over their objections.
the **ENEMY** to overcome	Isolation
some **EXAMPLES**	Nicodemus (John 3) Woman at the well (John 4)

OF EVANGELISM[4]

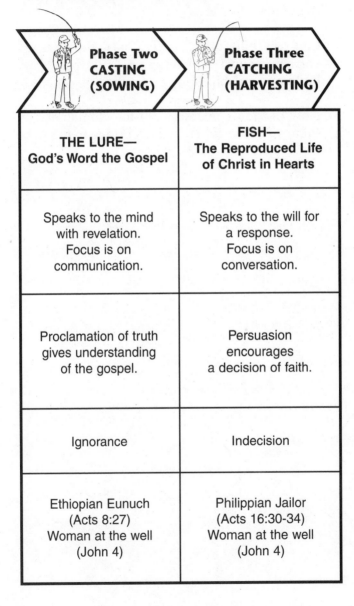

Phase Two CASTING (SOWING)	Phase Three CATCHING (HARVESTING)
THE LURE— God's Word the Gospel	FISH— The Reproduced Life of Christ in Hearts
Speaks to the mind with revelation. Focus is on communication.	Speaks to the will for a response. Focus is on conversation.
Proclamation of truth gives understanding of the gospel.	Persuasion encourages a decision of faith.
Ignorance	Indecision
Ethiopian Eunuch (Acts 8:27) Woman at the well (John 4)	Philippian Jailor (Acts 16:30-34) Woman at the well (John 4)

Personal Growth

- What does your personal lifestyle-evangelism process look like?

- Can you think of any individuals who have created barriers against the things of God? How can you build a friendship-bridge over their objections?

- How did Jesus interact with the woman at the well (John 4)? How did He build a bridge to her unbelief?

Chapter Thirteen

Fishing with the Disciples
"Your Net or Mine?"

Some of the greatest fishing stories ever written are found in the Holy Bible. If you were to embark on a fishing trip with the first-century disciples, you would not find them using a Quantum graphite rod with a high-retrieve Quantum 500-EX reel, and Stren super-tough fishing line. The equipment used by our fishing forefathers was crude but very effective.

Today, if you were to go to the House of Anchors at the Kibbutz Ein Gev, located on the eastern shoreline of the Sea of Galilee, you would find artifacts dating back to the time of Christ that clearly depict the type of fishing equipment that was available to the disciples. There is a great assortment of hooks, sinkers (stone and lead), line, nets, and boat anchors that help the modern-day angler connect with his spiritual and fishing roots.

The Sea of Galilee has 18 species of fish, ten of which are commercially important and represent a food source to the many communities surrounding the Sea of Galilee. This is true today just as it was during the time of Christ. In the Sea of Galilee one will find fish that resemble our tilapia (called musht), the ancient barbels fish, an ancient catfish, and several species of carp.

Very little fishing was done in biblical times with a hook and line because this method was not particularly effective or efficient. Today, as you roam the shores of the Sea of Galilee, you will find the majority of fishermen using the same netting strategies used 2,000 years ago.

The hook-and-line angler is a very unfamiliar scene, representing perhaps only one or two percent of the fishermen on the lake. Angling, as we know it, is only mentioned once in the Gospels, and then not in connection with ordinary fishing (Matthew 17:24-27). In this passage we find Peter being prodded by Jesus to go down to the shoreline and cast in his line. Peter's faith and God's miracle provided a specific fish with a silver coin in its mouth, which was used to pay the temple tax for both Jesus and himself.

I am indebted to Mendel Nun, the Homer Circle of Israel, for his thoughts regarding the netting strategies described below. He is recognized as a leading authority on ancient fishing techniques. The following techniques all relate in some way to specific teachings of Christ.

The Seine (Dragnet)

From the shores of Tabgha, a suburb of Capernaum, located on the northern shoreline, we find Christ describing to His disciples an allegory of the kingdom of heaven: "Once again, the kingdom of heaven is like a net that was let down into the lake and caught all kinds of fish. When it was full, the fishermen pulled it up on the shore. Then they sat down and collected the good fish in baskets, but threw the bad away" (Matthew 13:47-48).

This fits exactly the function of the seine or dragnet. The dragnet is made of netting shaped like a long wall, typically 250 to 300 yards long, and three to four yards high. Most often these nets were set early in the morning or late in the evening when the fish would frequent the shallow water areas.[1]

This netting technique could not be worked by a single man but required a group of fishermen. By attaching one end to the shoreline, the boat would make a large circle into the sea. The cork floats held the top of the net up in the water as the rock or lead weights pulled the bottom line of the net to the floor of the lake.

After all of the net was fed out the back of the boat, the fishermen would bring the remaining end back to shore, where another group of fishermen would take the line. As the two groups of shore fishermen pulled the net onto the bank, the enclosed area became smaller with each passing moment. The net moved through the water like a vertical wall bringing in a conglomerate of creatures. It was unforgiving, encompassing virtually everything in its sphere of reach.

After the net was dragged up on the shore, everything was sorted out by the handlers. This was a consuming and detailed task that required a great deal of accuracy. The good fish were put into vessels or baskets, sometimes with water to keep them fresh and alive for the marketplace. The "bad" fish—probably carp (because they were bony) and catfish (the Levitical law prohibited eating fish without scales [Leviticus 11:9])—were destroyed, not to be caught again.

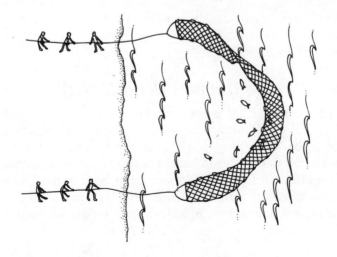

The Cast Net

Matthew 4:18 describes a person casting a net into the sea. The net referred to here—a "cast net"—is shaped like a large circle (six to eight yards in diameter) and could be used from the shore or a boat.

This net would be thrown into a spot where fish were thought to be congregating. As the net opened to its full circumference, the lead or rock weights on the perimeter of the circular net caused it to collapse around the unsuspecting fish. The bottom line was then drawn tight, entrapping the fish. Our Lord used this analogy to encourage His disciples to gather men for salvation and to become "fishers of men."[2]

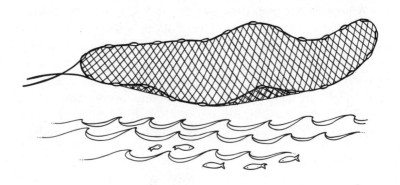

The Trammel Net (Gill Net)

The trammel net is the only one used in ancient times that is still predominant on the lake today. By intertwining three layers of netting, varying in mesh size, a long net is constructed that varies in height and length. It is constructed with a buoyant top line and weighted bottom line, thereby creating a wall that fish run into. This type of net requires a tremendous amount of mending and repair to keep it in proper shape.

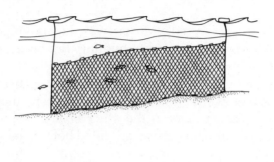

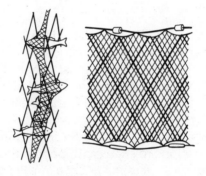

In the trammel net the very mesh becomes wrapped around the gills of the fish, causing them to suffocate and die within the net's grasp. The net is then retrieved, the fish are pulled from it, and then sorted accordingly. A good night's catch could bring up to 200 pounds of fish, if the net was properly located in a strategic area.

This type of net was used by the disciples in Luke 5:1-7:

> One day as Jesus was standing by the Lake of Gennesaret, with the people crowding around him and listening to the word of God, he saw at the water's edge two boats, left there by the fishermen, who were washing their nets. He got into one of the boats, the one belonging to Simon, and asked him to put out a little from shore. Then he sat down and taught the people from the boat.

> When he had finished speaking, he said to Simon, "Put out into deep water, and let down the nets for a catch."
>
> Simon answered, "Master, we've worked hard all night and haven't caught anything. But because you say so, I will let down the nets."
>
> When they had done so, they caught such a number of fish that their nets began to break. So they signaled their partners in the other boat to come and help them, and they came and filled both boats so full that they began to sink.[3] (See also John 21:1-9.)

Once again, I appreciate Christ's practical approach of communicating with His disciples. He relates His teachings to things that will be easily understood by those He is trying to reach. Though He was the most scholarly rabbi of His time, He did not try to become too theological or philosophical with these simple fishermen. Christ is always seen thinking of others.

As modern-day disciples, it is important that we use practical illustrations to share with people those basic truths that transform lives. *How and where will you cast your net?*

There are several styles and approaches to evangelism and discipleship, just as there are assorted nets to catch fish. Many books have been written that address the various techniques and strategies involved. At the risk of oversimplifying the subject, I would like to suggest that there are at least three styles that are being used by Christians today.

To some degree we can see these evangelistic styles represented in the kinds of nets used by our ancient fishermen friends.

The Entrapment Method: Trammel Net

You invite an unsaved friend to a Christian event without telling him there will be some intense preaching as part of the program. You have driven him and his family to the event and have lost your keys in the parking lot. The pay phone is out of order and the church doors have been locked.

The two greeters at the back of the room are six-foot-eight and look like unhappy Hulk Hogans. There is no way for your visitors to escape—*they are trapped.*

In an effort to be cordial, the pastor, who is dressed up in a heavily starched white shirt with a tie from the 1970s, asks your guests to stand up and introduce themselves to the crowd. Just after your friends have mopped up the puddle of perspiration from around their chairs, the usher sticks an offering plate in their face and suggests that a gift would be in order.

Do we wonder why these neighbors never speak to us again and have placed a pit bull in their front yard?

A little absurd? Perhaps! But often in our passion to "save souls" we do not think through how our customs may offend, frighten, or even disengage a person searching for truth. Evangelical pastors from "seeker sensitive churches" tell us that the two most threatening things a "newcomer" can be asked to do is to address a group of strangers and to give away their money. Let's face it: the potential for intimidation in certain churches is great.

Large church events certainly have their place, but they often fail to yield positive results with unsuspecting friends who do not know Jesus. To many of these people the entrapment process feels like the trammel net described earlier. The unsuspecting visitor swims into a net of excitement and programs that end up strangling him or her into submission or death. Most often any decisions made in this setting are short-lived and insincere at best.

Encourage your church to plan outreach events that present a comfortable, relaxed atmosphere. It is always good to use the outdoor environment or a community facility whenever possible. These are the least threatening and most comfortable places for the unbeliever. You can then gradually introduce them to your church facilities.

Avoid structured presentations and make sure there are plenty of happy, joyful Christians who can be introduced to your friends. Make it a point to know your guest's occupation, hobbies, and interests. Find someone in your church who shares those experiences and make sure they have some informal time to talk with one another.

You should take responsibility for introducing your visitors to others. And be sure to mention to your visitors that *they are your guests* and should not worry about putting anything in the offering basket—*that is for church members only.*

If your visitors feel you have been protective of their interests, they will be more receptive to an invitation to attend another program—perhaps even coming to church to meet that "cool pastor" they met at the casting pond.

The Smothering Method: Cast Net

In our zeal to see a lost one saved, we develop an encompassing strategy that surrounds the unbeliever with considerable information and confrontations. We are sure to buy him or her a copy of the latest book on salvation while weekly encouraging him or her to attend church with us.

Our unbelieving friends often feel trapped and engulfed. They try to be kind and keep us as friends, but they can't stand our religiosity. Moreover, our inconsistent walk gets in the way of a reasonable evaluation of God's Word.

Much like the cast net described earlier in the chapter, unbelievers are always looking for the net to be flung and the smothering to occur. Their best defense is to keep a healthy distance from anyone who might be a suspected "fisherman."

People can sense insincerity. If you are fellowshipping with them simply to "save a soul," your phoniness will eventually surface and you will be discovered. People must first learn to love and respect us; *then* we have earned the right to share the love of Jesus with them.

The Sane Method: Seine (Dragnet)

There is a sane way to approach discipleship and lifestyle evangelism. Throughout this book we have talked about the essence of discipleship. We must be models of the truth. It is our genuine love and concern that will first attract people's attention. We encourage their further exploration and consideration by being available and providing encouragement as opportunities present themselves.

We must remember that people will accept Jesus into their hearts when they see the value of a personal relationship with the living God. When they realize the emptiness in their lives and the lack of a cementing agent to hold their family together, *then* they are ready to be counseled and instructed on the biblical truths that transform.

The seine (dragnet) approach to capturing fish is by far the most forgiving and humane. The net is *slowly* moved around the fish to avoid scaring them. As the net is drawn closer to the fish, they have the freedom to jump over the net and escape. The caring fisherman usually leaves enough net in the water that a pool of live fish is left for sorting. Should the net reach the shoreline with the captured fish, there exists a chance for the fish to be returned to the sea.

Of course, it is not up to us to pass judgment on any individual. We are simply tools in the hands of the Master, being used to help shape and encourage others in their spiritual growth. The prodding of the Holy Spirit is the primary motivating agent in the process.

Determining the Spiritual Temperature

I met Jay Carty, former NBA star, at a Professional Athletes Outreach program several years ago. Jay has written several very enjoyable books and is frequently on the speaking circuit. He shared an interesting truth about our "spiritual temperature" that bears some ink.

If we could grade a person's soul from a -10 to a +10 we would make the following assumptions:

At the -10 level we would find Satan himself. At a -9 level we would probably find someone like Adolf Hitler. If we looked across to the other side of the spectrum we would find Jesus Christ representing a +10. Perhaps someone like Billy Graham or Mother Teresa would represent a +9. In the middle, at ground zero, is the cross—*a new creature* ("Therefore, if anyone is in Christ, he is a new creation; the old has gone, the new has come!"—2 Corinthians 5:17). This would be the point in time at which a person accepts the Lord Jesus Christ as Savior.

If we agree that people are always in process, then you can imagine folks maturing and developing along this axis in varying degrees. For those who continue in sin and promote the evil side of humankind, they will tend to move toward the -10 as their hearts become hardened and their lustful appetites devour their sense of goodness. However, most lost souls tend to move toward the cross (new creature) as they interact with true disciples and life experiences that show them their need for a loving Savior.

We never really know where on that axis a searching soul lies. Our encouragement and support may have moved a person from a -7 to a -6. Someone else comes along and moves them to a -5. And finally, someday, an event or an encounter occurs that brings them to the point of salvation.

These are the people we most often hear giving their testimonies during a baptismal ceremony. They testify that their lives have been changing over the course of time and suddenly they come to accept the truth set before them. *How did you come to accept Jesus?*

How to Establish and Maintain a Good Relationship with the New or "Pre" Christian

If you are serious about making discipleship a part of your personal ministry, it is important to adhere to some basic practices that can help you attain dramatic results. The disciple-fishermen of the first century were successful with their nets because they knew how to use them effectively. The nets worked because of the meticulous preparation provided ahead of time. Careful attention was given to mending, restoring, and setting the nets. So it must be with discipleship—*we must prepare ourselves ahead of time*. Constant prayer and forethought are required to be successful at fishing for souls.

DETERMINING THE SPIRITUAL TEMPERATURE [4]

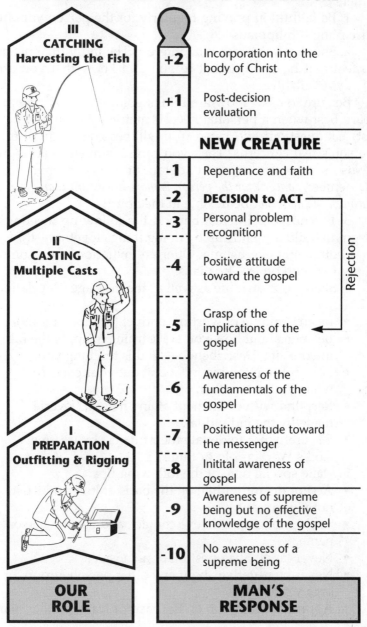

OUR ROLE		MAN'S RESPONSE
III **CATCHING** Harvesting the Fish	**+2**	Incorporation into the body of Christ
	+1	Post-decision evaluation
		NEW CREATURE
	-1	Repentance and faith
	-2	**DECISION to ACT**
	-3	Personal problem recognition
II **CASTING** Multiple Casts	**-4**	Positive attitude toward the gospel
	-5	Grasp of the implications of the gospel
	-6	Awareness of the fundamentals of the gospel
	-7	Positive attitude toward the messenger
I **PREPARATION** Outfitting & Rigging	**-8**	Initial awareness of gospel
	-9	Awareness of supreme being but no effective knowledge of the gospel
	-10	No awareness of a supreme being

Rejection

The following suggestions may be helpful as you disciple others:

1. Be faithful in praying regularly for the person you are discipling (Philippians 4:6).

2. Show genuine personal interest. The individual needs to feel that he is important to you and know that you are always available.

Be sure to ask, "How are things going for you?" People learn best when a personal need is met. As you show interest, ask questions and listen. You will become aware of this person's real concerns. Then you can sensitively share how Jesus is relevant to every detail of every human life. Remember, *concern for the person is more important than getting through the material*. Be flexible in the Spirit!

3. Extend your interest beyond the follow-up meetings. Begin to build a friendship by doing things together—things you both enjoy like fishing. Offer an invitation to do something fun with other Christians.

4. Share your own life as well as the message (Revelation 12:11).

- Be an example of worthy conduct (Philippians 4:9).
- Be open about how you are learning to apply the Bible in your life. Describe what God is teaching you.
- Be natural in talking to God about your concerns when you're together.
- Respond with excitement at any new discoverie made by the individual.
- Be careful not to deflate their interest by treating God's Word as old or familiar.

5. Make special note of the following tips:

- Accept the individual on the basis of love and trust, not performance.
- Smile a lot, maintain eye contact, and use the person's name.
- Never laugh at a question or an answer.
- Never be negative about any other person, group, or organization.
- Approach follow-up on the basis of *sharing* rather than

teaching (Philippians 2:3-4). Admit when you do not know an answer. Look it up together or find the answer later.

- *Be enthusiastic.* Your attitude is contagious.

6. If the individual does not have a modern translation of the Bible, offer to loan one of yours, or go together to a bookstore to buy one.

Personal Growth

- What form of evangelism do you wish to adopt as your style, and why?

- If you do not know Christ as your personal Savior, where would you place yourself on the "Spiritual Temperature" graph? What will it take to move you to the center (new creature)?

- Could you feel comfortable asking someone you're trying to lead to the Lord if they could articulate where they are in their spiritual journey?

- What does it mean to be a new creature? Read 2 Corinthians 5:17.

Drawn to the Light
"Considering the Ultimate Question"

Tucked away in the 27th chapter of Matthew is a question that was raised by Pontius Pilate to a crowd of onlookers in the court of his palace. The question is the same one that every person must ultimately answer: "What shall I do, then, with Jesus who is called Christ?" (Matthew 27:22).

The background leading up to this infamous inquiry may be found in John 8. Jesus entered Jerusalem for the last time. Here He spent about six months teaching others about His identity and mission. Jerusalem had to evaluate and react to His claim to be the promised Messiah—God from heaven, the Redeemer of humankind.

Early in John's Gospel Jesus was the "light of men" (John 1:4). In keeping with this, during His last months of ministry, Jesus boldly proclaimed His deity and asked people to follow Him, saying, "I am the light of the world; he who follows Me shall not walk in the darkness, but shall have the light of life" (8:12 NASB).

Of course, many then as now refuse to come to the Light of the world. The reason is simple. As Jesus explained in John

3:19-20, men love darkness instead of light because their deeds are evil.

In any event, during the Feast of Tabernacles, when the large golden lamp stands were lit after the evening sacrifice, Jesus gathered people in the temple courtyard to announce that He was a light from God that lights the way for life. He was much like the pillar of fire that illuminated the way for the Israelites in the wilderness (Exodus 13:21). All who follow Christ will walk in the light and are recipients of eternal life.

John the Baptist earlier proclaimed that "he was not that light, but was sent to bear witness of that light" (John 1:8 KJV). Jesus' message pointed the way to a spiritual awakening and to eternal life by believing in the "light of life" (verse 12).

The choice the people had to make was whether to receive Him for who He claimed to be, or, by rejection, to join those who crucified Him. That ultimate question still faces us today. Each person must decide for or against Christ. Turning our backs—or even just ignoring the question—results in living in darkness.

The Glorious Light of Christ

Cotton Cordell, a close friend of mine, has a fascinating story he tells relating to the biblical teaching that "Jesus is the light." I met this top Bassmaster fisherman and lure manufacturer in 1967. He has a wonderful spirit and a sensitive heart that has endeared him to thousands of fans across America. His innovative designs and marketing ideas have long captivated the fishing industry.

For many years Cotton and I worked together in promoting his Cordell Spot Lures and the legendary fat-bodied "Big O's" named after Otis Young. The inventor of this popular bait was Fred Young, Otis's brother, a disabled fisherman who loved to carve and whittle custom lures for fishermen. Cotton tells me that he met ol' Fred whittling plugs on his front porch during the summer of 1972.

The Big O's were famous with local fishermen and were

being rented out by Otis for up to 50 dollars per day. Their fish-catching qualities were directly associated with the unique design. Cotton and Fred soon struck a deal that allowed Fred to retire and placed Cordell lures at the top of the industry.

Cotton and I built a strong appreciation for each other over the years. His unabashed love of the Lord is a trait he is most proud of.

During a local sports show, we had a chance to present a prayer breakfast for a group of exhibitors. Cotton shared a story about Jesus as the "light of the world" that I will never forget.

Cotton and his wife have two children. When the children were young and jobs were scarce, Cotton fed and clothed the family by catching and selling shad bait.

Shad are best caught at night. Like many other fish, shad are attracted to light. Cotton used this fact to his advantage. He recalls,

> I simply put a garbage can in the middle of the boat and hired a boy to run the motor (a ten-horsepower Johnson) and hold a light on the water by the side of the boat. He steered the boat with one hand and shined the light with the other.
>
> We ran the boat at a slow trolling speed while standing on the front deck with a long-handled net made of chicken wire. The shad chased the light alongside the boat and I scooped them up in the net.
>
> I experienced the same thing when fishing for crappie on Lake Hamilton or speckled trout in the Gulf of Mexico. I know fish can be drawn to a light. I believe those first-century disciples knew that too, except they didn't have a Coleman lantern to shine on the water. Knowing how creative those disciples were, I believe they built a fire in an iron bucket in the front of the boat and reflected the light into the water using a highly polished piece of bronze. The light drew the fish into their waiting nets.

However, the brightest light wasn't the result of any fire the disciples made. I believe the light of the Savior is what drew the fish to Him and into the disciples' nets. We read in Exodus 33 how Moses experienced the power of God's light. The face of Moses shone for days after he met God. We also read how Paul encountered Christ on the road to Damascus and was blinded by the light of Christ (Acts 9).

I think the reason the disciples didn't catch a fish until Jesus told them to cast out their nets toward the shoreline (the right side of the boat) in John 21 was that the brilliance of Christ had attracted every fish in the sea to the area where He waited for the disciples. Surely you wouldn't expect ordinary fishermen to compete with the "Light of Jesus Christ"!

Four Lessons on Discipling

In his book *The Uttermost Star*, F. W. Boreham quotes a rhyme that provides four tips on how to catch fish. This rhyme is well known among fly-rod fishermen, who must be more mindful of details and presentation than other types of anglers. Here it is:

> Be sure your face is toward the light;
> Study the fish's curious ways;
> Then keep yourself well out of sight,
> And cherish patience all your days.[1]

I believe there are at least four lessons we can learn about discipling from fly fishermen. The lessons are encapsulated in the above rhyme.

Lesson One: Face the Sun (Son)

If you want to catch fish, face the sun. This will eliminate the possibility of spooking the fish with your shadow. Fish will often feed facing the sun so they can see the shadows of the insect-life floating on top of the water in contrast to the bright sun.

If your desire is to impress people with the love and grace of our Lord, you must have a radiant face. You must be willing to allow the joy in your heart to shine forth. A good pastor will pick ushers and greeters who understand this principle and who are in love with people. Their zeal for life and their gracious spirit are a blessing to those coming to church for encouragement and support.

Jesus said, "Let your light shine before men, that they may see your good deeds and praise your Father in heaven" (Matthew 5:16). How can we be more joyful about our faith? A flashlight (a soul) is not effective until you put some strong batteries (the Holy Spirit) into the compartment. Maybe the reason your flashlight does not work well is that you forgot to put in the batteries. Like the disciples, we all need to be filled with the Holy Spirit (Acts 2:4). A "fruit" of the Holy Spirit is joy (Galatians 5:22).

Lesson Two: Study the "Fish"

No one should claim to be a good fisherman if he has only studied the rods, reels, lines, lures, and flies. If you want to be an effective fisherman (*or* disciple), you must carefully study every aspect of the "fish." You need to know their habits, habitat, moods, responses, and attitudes. You need to observe the creature in its environment. You need to study its ways. Then you know better what approach to take with them.

You must also know your enemy—*Satan*. You need to be aware of how he can cause you or the one you are discipling to stumble or fall. You must anticipate his cunning ways and vicious attacks. "Be self-controlled and alert. Your enemy the devil prowls around like a roaring lion looking for someone to devour" (1 Peter 5:8).

Lesson Three: Keep a Low Profile

Most good fly fishermen approach the water in a quiet manner, keeping low to the ground to avoid giving away their position. They want to keep their image from the fish so that the complete concentration of the fish is on the fly. I prefer to wear camouflaged clothing to further promote a stealthlike appearance.

A disciple who is keenly aware of God's purpose in his life will not try to center attention on himself. Moreover, one who is discipling others will want those under him to focus upon God's Word and the Lord Jesus instead of himself. The most respected pastors and teachers rarely use the word "I," but give God the credit and the primary focus of their attention.

Jesus spoke about keeping a low profile in Matthew 6:1: "Be careful not to do your 'acts of righteousness' before men, to be seen by them. If you do, you will have no reward from your Father in heaven."

Lesson Four: Be Patient

The fisherman who patiently waits for that illusive nibble is the one who will ultimately become the victor. Sometimes fish just do not want to bite. Rather than give up, keep casting and try new approaches.

Our responsibility as a disciple is to be faithful to our Lord and attentive to the Holy Spirit (Galatians 5:16). We are responsible to *be available*, to present the Word of God, and *live it* through our lives (James 1:22).

The Holy Spirit has the responsibility of preparing a person's heart and capturing his or her spirit (John 16:8-11). We cannot claim any victory for ourselves. *It is His and His alone.*

As we keep these facts in mind, it will be easier for us to maintain patience as we engage in fishing for men. And as we continue to fish for men, the ultimate question they must face continues to be, "What shall I do, then, with Jesus who is called Christ?" (Matthew 27:22).

Personal Growth

- How are you answering the age-old question, "What shall I do, then, with Jesus who is called Christ?" (Matthew 27:22)

- How do you recharge your spiritual batteries?

- What does "being self-controlled and alert" mean to you? (1 Peter 5:8)

Chapter Fifteen

Fellowship
"Joining a Fishing Club"

One of the best ways to become a good fisherman is to surround yourself with others who enjoy the sport as much as you do and who are willing to share information that will enhance your abilities. In 1968 I started fishing several regional tournaments. Because tournament bass fishing was such a new sport, only a few of my friends were knowledgeable on the strategies required to excel at it.

By and by, I met other East Bay area people who shared my passion for bass fishing. We decided it would be beneficial if we could meet outside the confines of a tournament to have some close fellowship. In 1970 we chartered the Castro Valley Bass Classics which, to this day, continues to meet monthly to help fishermen become more skilled and introduce others to the joys of fishing.

We all realized there is more to fishing than buying the right clothes and tackle, or zipping around a lake in a fancy bass boat. Meeting regularly with others allows you to learn new and different ideas that can be verified in your own experience. To be an effective fisherman, you must constantly educate yourself on new techniques and be willing to put your line into the water to test those theories. Merely looking the part does not make you a fisherman.

My friend Hank Parker told me a story about his own embarrassing moment of "looking the part." Hank had been doing many shows and seminars and not much fishing. He had just received his new Ranger bass boat and decided to take it and all his new tackle out to Lake Bisten in Louisiana to do some filming.

As he was launching his boat, he noticed two "good ol' boys" in their old beat-up, wooden boat watching his every move. Hank said, "You could see the envy in their faces as they looked me over."

It turned out that Hank had a very tough day and did not catch a single fish. Late that evening, he motored up to the dock and started loading his boat on the trailer.

Just then, the "good ol' boys" showed up waving a big stringer of fish at Hank. They asked, "How did you do?"

Hank had to admit his utter frustration and failure.

The two men said, "Boy, you sure looked good goin' out, but you're lookin' bad comin' back!"

Many disciples have a similar problem. They get all dressed up in their best outfits, carry around their fancy leather-bound Bibles, and say all the right things as they participate in Sunday services. They have the right look. But in the end there are no spiritual results. Come Monday morning, it's back to the old way of life. Many disciples fail to take advantage of the benefits associated with committed participation in Christian fellowship.

Some churches are not much better. They have beautiful architecture, numerous pastors, great choirs, and assorted programs to make sure that folks come to their church. But these same churches fail to follow the Great Commission and wonder why the people in their congregations sit passively in their pews week in and week out.

As Bill Hull put it in his book *Jesus Christ, Disciple Maker*,

Many Christians think of themselves as an audience to be entertained rather than an army ready to march. The first-century church, composed of a tiny band of committed people, brought the mighty Roman world to its knees. In the twentieth century, however, it often seems that we who are many in the church have allowed the worldly culture to disciple us into its way of thinking.[1]

A church should be a place of fellowship for disciples who wish to grow in *their own* faith while being equipped to reach *others* with the good news of the gospel. Much like a family or a fishing club, a church fellowship can provide encouragement and support. It should be a place free of conflict and condemnation. A fellowship should stimulate an individual to new levels of confidence and commitment.

Fishless Fishermen

Some churchgoers have missed the real purpose of a church fellowship. They believe that attendance alone is sufficient for membership. Likewise, many disciples fail to realize that fishing for men is a process that requires a real commitment. If the church is to be successful in attracting others to join, then church members must be willing to grab a rod (a Bible), get a buddy (fellowship), and get a line wet (disciple others).

Lorne Sanny, a Navigator associate, summarizes my concern best in his story about the "Fishless Fishermen." Listen to his words:

There was a group called Fishermen's Fellowship. They were surrounded by streams and lakes full of hungry fish. They met regularly to discuss the call to fish, the abundance of fish, and the thrill of catching fish. They got excited about fishing.

Someone suggested they needed a philosophy of fishing. So they carefully defined and redefined fishing strategies and tactics.

Then they realized they had been going at it backwards. They had approached fishing from the point of view of fishermen and not from the point of view of the fish. How do fish view the world? How does the fisherman appear to the fish? What do fish eat and when? These are all good things to know.

So they began research studies and attended conferences on fishing. Some traveled to faraway places to study different kinds of fish with different habits. Some got PhDs in fishiology. But no one had yet gone fishing.

So a committee was formed to send out fishermen. As prospective fishing places outnumbered the fishermen, the committee needed to determine priorities. A priority list of fishing places was posted on bulletin boards in all the Fellowship Halls.

Still no one was fishing. A survey was launched to find out why. Most did not answer the questionnaire but from those who did respond, it was discovered that some felt called to study fish, a few to furnish fishing equipment, and several to go around encouraging fishermen. What with meetings, conferences, and seminars, others simply didn't have time to fish.

Jake was a newcomer to the Fishermen's Fellowship. After one stirring meeting of the Fellowship, Jake went fishing. He tried a few things, got the hang of it, and caught a choice fish. At the next meeting, he told his story, was honored for his catch, and was then scheduled to speak at all the Fellowship chapters and tell how he did it.

Now because of all the speaking and his election to the Board of Directors of the Fishermen's Fellowship, Jake no longer had time to go fishing.

Soon he began to feel restless and empty. He longed to feel the tug on the line once again. He cut the speaking, resigned from the Board, and said to a friend, "Let's go fishing." They did—just the two of them—and they caught fish.

The members of the Fishermen's Fellowship were many, the fish were plentiful, but the fishers were few.[2]

What type of Fishermen's Fellowship do you attend? Have you been fishing lately or are you one of the "want-to-bes" or "groupies?" Is your fishing club guided by the Great Commission (Matthew 28:19) or the Great Spectator Syndrome?

This book is written to the true Fishermen's Fellowship—the church—made up of disciples who use their God-given talents in the marketplace of life. Because work environments, social contacts, academic institutions, and friendships are uniquely different for every believer, there is a host of contacts awaiting each disciple-fisherman.

What Attracts People to the Church?

All too often we mistakenly think that the reason people are attracted to our fellowships is because of external issues. Is our church big enough? Do we have enough parking? Can the pastor really put out a great message every Sunday? Does our choir have the right outfits? Do we have enough programs for the kids?

In reality your friends will be attracted to your church because *they were first attracted to you and your spirit-filled life.* Does this surprise you?

A survey was conducted that asked Christians, "Who had the greatest influence on your life for Christ?" The survey listed various traits and qualities. Responses included statements such as, "Was he a great theologian?" "Was he a dynamic person?" "Did he impress you with his knowledge and wisdom?" "Was he good looking?" "Did he have power and wealth?"

The results of the survey are highly revealing. Most people suggested that the key qualities included:

- He cared for me.
- He believed in me.
- He took time to listen to me.
- He had a close walk with God.

Jim Petersen, in his wonderful book *Lifestyle Discipleship*, talks about the role of the church and the disciple. Consider his words:

> Traditionally we have assumed we can discharge our responsibilities to the unbelievers by somehow attracting them to come into our churches. A certain percentage will come, but it is obvious that the main-stream will pass us by. This heightens the importance of the person we are calling the "insider." Insiders are Christians who see a person's everyday arena of life as the logical place of ministry....The church is a people gathered unto Christ and sent into the world.... If insiders are indeed central to God's purposes for the church, then it follows that our needs for being equipped and resourced deserve the highest priority.[3]

Communities of Fellowship

Churches are gathering places we call communities. Webster defines community as "a group of people living together as a smaller social unit within a larger one, and having interests, work, and so on, in common."

We are all part of many communities. We have neighborhood associations that are part of an even larger community called a city, which is part of an even larger community called a state, and so on. If you are part of a Sunday school class or are a church member, then you are part of a community—*a fellowship of believers*.

The fishermen-apostle John was familiar with kibbutz (community settlement) living. He lived in Capernaum located along the shores of the Sea of Galilee and saw the fruits of strong fellowship. In his first epistle he spoke of the fellowship we have with God:

We proclaim to you what we have seen and heard, so that you also may have fellowship with us. And our fellowship is with the father and with his Son, Jesus Christ. . . . God is light; in him there is no darkness at all. If we claim to have fellowship with him yet walk in the darkness, we lie and do not live by the truth. But if we walk in the light, as he is in the light, we have fellowship with one another, and the blood of Jesus, his Son, purifies us from all sin. (1 John 1:3,5-7)

First and foremost, then, we must have fellowship with the Father. Fellowship is a "living bond" or a "mutual abiding." Jesus modeled this quality for His disciples by the way He related to His Father. He said, "The Son can do nothing by himself; he can do only what he sees his Father doing, because whatever the Father does, the Son also does. For the Father loves the Son and shows him all he does" (John 5:19).

Much like Christ's relationship to the Father, there is a special interdependence that exists among those associated within a church fellowship. Jesus' disciples readily accepted this familiar concept because their lives as fishermen virtually depended on teamwork. They counted on each other. Some worked to make the boats and nets ready; others strained at pulling on the oars; others helped set the nets; and still others pulled the end lines from shore.

Much like a fishing village in the time of Jesus, an effective church ministry uses all the gifts and talents of its members. They have a genuine love and concern for others. The fellowship is motivated to reach out into the world with a caring and serving heart.

Reaching Outsiders

We should be interested in building bridges to the unbeliever. Too often churchgoers seem to concentrate on those things that separate us from someone who is seeking Christ. Sometimes we allow certain behaviors and appearances to become barriers to our calling. Perhaps that person sitting on the sidelines of life is just waiting for someone to extend the hand of fellowship.

People come to church fellowships because they see an open, authentic disciple who cares for and loves them unconditionally. According to a 1978 Gallup poll, 41 percent of the people sampled indicated they were unchurched. In 1988, 44 percent indicated the same. The most interesting statistic is that of these same unchurched people, 58 percent said they would consider attending church if they were asked properly.

Bill Hull makes an important observation regarding this point:

> Jesus demonstrated that fishing for men means going where they are. If people feel accepted, then they will relax and open up, which would be very unlikely if a judgmental attitude were communicated to them. Some of the most open people, whose hungry hearts are ripe for the gospel, smoke, curse, and tell off-color jokes.[4]

The Christian who desires to reach outsiders must be willing to encounter some corruption and adversity. I do not advocate participation in such unholy activity, but neither do I promote total isolation from it.

The more moderate track of a *critical presence* is advised. A mature Christian can survive in such an atmosphere on a limited basis and still not practice or condone questionable activities.

An effective fisherman takes every opportunity to fish in *promising waters*. He casts into unknown waters with an expectant heart and looks for opportunities to challenge the fish with the techniques and approaches learned at the fishing club meeting. By being patient, he pursues his quarry with a discerning spirit.

If he is to become a better fisherman, he does not wait until he has mastered the sport before he begins to fish. He uses the abilities he presently has within the environment he places himself. If he only fished a trout pond with planted fish, his skills would never improve.

Dr. Haddon Robinson, president of Denver Conservative Baptist Seminary, and one who strongly believes in lifestyle evangelism, summarizes his view this way:

> Making a place in your life for non-Christian neighbors demands effort, thought, and at times risk. Bridges are harder to construct than walls. But that doesn't alter reality: Outsiders to faith are first drawn to Christians and then to Christ. Unfortunately, not all Christians attract. Like a turned magnet, some repel. Yet Christians, alive to God, loving, caring, laughing, sharing, involved at the point of people's need, present an undeniable witness for Christ in their society.[5]

Evangelism is not an optional accessory to a Christian. *It is the heartbeat of a disciple's life.* The commission of our churches should give meaning to all else undertaken in the name of Christ. As Robert E. Coleman put it,

> The Great Commission of Christ given to his church is summed up in the command to "make disciples of every creature" (Matthew 28:19). The word here indicates that the disciples were to go out into the world and win others who would come to be what they themselves were—disciples of Christ.[6]

Your Relationship to the Church

Having shown the importance of lifestyle evangelism to draw people *into* the church, it is now important to understand the nature of our relationship to the church. Toward this end, I want to suggest three concepts a disciple should remember about church fellowships—the need for submission to Christ, the mutual dependence of church members, and the need for accountability. Let's take a brief look at these.

Submission to Christ

The first thing we see with Christ's fishing disciples is that they were *willing to be directed*. They listened to the call of discipleship, evaluated it with a submissive spirit, and practiced those learned character qualities that would please the Savior and separate them from the world system.

If we are to be effective Christians, we need to be obedient to the call and follow him (Matthew 4:18-22; Luke 5:10). Our fellowships can help us learn more about God and His plan for our lives. At church we can become equipped as disciples (Ephesians 4:11-12).

We also need to keep in mind that people searching to know more about Christ can use a church service as a "come and see" opportunity. First, though, *they must be invited*. That's where you and I come into the picture. We can invite outsiders to a church fellowship.

Mutual Dependence

A second concept that is important to grasp about church fellowships is that members are to be dependent on each other. By sharing gifts and talents, fishing for men becomes easier. When a team is involved in a mission, the load becomes lighter and the challenges less threatening. The disciples were sent out in pairs (Mark 6:7)—for protection, encouragement, accountability, and companionship, but most of all *to support one another with their gifts*.

Jesus was dependent upon the Father and the Father was dependent upon the Son to fulfill His plan. The disciples were dependent upon Christ and He upon them to empower the first-century church. Today, we need each other and the Holy Spirit to help us expand the kingdom.

The nature of a dependent relationship suggests that we remain flexible and open to new information and biblical teachings. The similarities between fishing and discipling are once again seen.

When I was refining my tournament fishing skills, I tried to remain open and flexible to new techniques. Many of my friends loved to boast, "I'm a jig man," or "I'm a worm fisherman," or "I would not be caught dead fishing anything but a level wind reel." The secret to being a good fisherman is to remain open and flexible. Learn to fish *all* the baits well, so you can respond to the fish under any given circumstance.

The first-century disciples remained flexible and open to new ideas. They did not let their ritualistic training and Jewish traditions get in the way of their work with the Lord. When Jesus had a better idea on how to fish (Luke 5; John 21), *they listened*. They left the comfort of their own thinking to try faith in Christ's teachings.

Most important, the disciple-fishermen went with Christ to the marketplace of life—the streets where the prostitutes congregated, the sickbeds of the lepers, the hillsides to find the demon-possessed, and the fishing villages to seek out the frustrated, lonely anglers. *Modern disciples are called to do the same.*

The Need for Accountability

Finally, a disciple must remain accountable to others. A caring, loving fellowship will provide the encouragement and interest in a member to ask the tough questions of life. To the degree that a disciple is open to constructive criticism and review, the fellowship should be willing to help evaluate his or her vision, attitudes, and practices. This is especially important to the new believer who does not yet know enough to reject the wrong and choose the right (Isaiah 7:15).

During the past 20 years, our society has seen many great leaders fall. A president was forced to resign his office because of a scandal. Two major television evangelists fell from grace because of greed and moral indiscretions. Too often we hear about a community leader who became so intoxicated with his power or position that he failed to heed the warning signals of a deteriorating family life and lost the most precious gift of all—*his family*.

When I hear about these kinds of things, I look beyond the person and ask the question, "Where was the board member or close friend who should have been challenging the person with penetrating observations at the beginning of the ordeal?" Ultimately, we are all responsible to God (Romans 3:19). But wise words and encouragement from a fellow believer are of great benefit to any person truly interested in seeking after God's heart (Proverbs 27:6). Accountability to others is an important safeguard for all of us!

If we are to benefit from fellowship, then, we should remain obedient, dependent, and accountable. Together we learn to share, taking full advantage of one another's gifts and talents. A fellowship provides opportunities to be discipled *and* to disciple others.

Let's remember that it is not enough to merely talk about fishing; *we all need to drop a line into the water.* "The harvest is plentiful, but the workers are few. Ask the Lord of the harvest, therefore, to send out workers into his harvest field" (Luke 10:2).

Personal Growth

- What is the primary objective for a church according to Jesus? (See Matthew 28:19; John 20:21; and Acts 1:8)

- Take an objective look at your church or Christian ministry. Compare its objectives to that of Christ's teaching. Are you just a spectator watching others fish, or are you experiencing the adventure?

- How can you become a more effective fisherman (disciple)?

- Find someone to disciple you. If you are a mature believer, look for someone to disciple.

Postscript: An Eternal Perspective

Earlier in the book I told you about my 9-½-hour surgery to remove a tumor from my brain. Because of God's grace and miraculous power, the surgery was completely successful.

By allowing me to live, I knew God was not finished with me. After six weeks and much therapy, I could see clearly and walk again. I returned to life knowing that God was giving me the opportunity to become all He wanted me to be. There would be no more wasted time. My priorities were now what they should be.

My experience in the hospital gave me a new appreciation for those who do not yet know Jesus Christ as their personal Savior. When you are at death's doorstep, the issue of where you want to spend eternity is of utmost concern. You give deep and reflective thought to who will be joining you and to those close friends and relatives who have not yet accepted God's saving grace.

It must have been much the same way for our Lord Jesus in His last days as He made special efforts to talk about heaven and hell. During His last days, He carefully explained three separate parables about heaven.

Even as I write, my Bible is open to Matthew 13:47-52 where our Lord used an analogy centered on a fishing experience to help the disciples understand more about one's destiny in the afterlife. In this parable, many fish have been captured in a net. When it was filled, the fishermen gathered out the good fish and put them into containers. The bad fish, however, were thrown away. This image graphically depicts God's separation of the righteous from the wicked at the end of the age.

This brings to mind the seine net mentioned in an earlier chapter. Recall that the netting technique for a seine net could not be worked by a single man but required a group of fishermen. By attaching one end to the shoreline, the boat would make a large circle into the sea. The cork floats held the top of the net up in the water as the rock or lead weights pulled the bottom line of the net to the floor of the lake.

After all of the net was fed out of the back of the boat, the fishermen would bring the remaining end back to shore, where a group of fishermen would take the line. As the two groups of shore fishermen pulled the net onto the bank, the enclosed area became smaller with each passing moment. The net moved through the water like a vertical wall bringing in a conglomerate of creatures. It was unforgiving, encompassing virtually everything in its sphere of reach.

After the net was dragged up on shore, everything was sorted out by the handlers. This was a consuming and detailed task that required a great deal of accuracy. The good fish were put into vessels or baskets, sometimes with water to keep them fresh and alive for the marketplace. The bad fish—probably carp (because they were bony) and catfish (the Levitical law prohibited eating fish without scales [Leviticus 11:9])—were destroyed, not to be caught again.[1]

Our Lord told His disciples that the final judgment will be like the seine netting experience. There will be a final separation of the righteous from the wicked in much the same way that good fish are separated from bad fish.

God temporarily tolerates evil in this sinful world. There will be a time, however, when the final judgment comes and evil will not be a part of His new kingdom. As the net moves slowly and silently through the sea of life, it is nondiscriminating, drawing men to the shore of eternity. By the time most people awaken to the reality of their sinful life, it will be too late.

Like fish in a dragnet, men are regularly touched by the gospel of Christ or the possibility of death through a "close call." However, the nature of man is to dart back into what he thinks is freedom. Unfortunately, he runs right back into another part of the net. Despite what New Agers and Hindus might say, there is no escape from the final judgment. The temporary freedom experienced within the vain philosophies of deceit ultimately lead to a suffocating death. Scripture tells us,

> This is how it will be at the end of the age. The angels will come and separate the wicked from the righteous and throw them into the fiery furnace, where there will be weeping and gnashing of teeth. (Matthew 13:49-50)

Our Lord was so concerned that His disciples understood these matters that He asked them, "Have you understood all these things?" (Matthew 13:51). Likewise, Jesus asks each of us, "Have you understood all these things?"

Do we understand that it is only through God's grace and a personal relationship with the Lord Jesus Christ that we can have eternal life (John 3:16-21)? Do we understand that it is through the sacrificial death of Jesus that our sins can be forgiven (Romans 3:24-25). God patiently stands ready to accept us. Our Lord is "long-suffering toward us, not willing that any should perish but that all should come to repentance" (2 Peter 3:9 NKJV).

The Attitude of a Disciple

Realizing these truths, what should our attitude be toward discipling? After our Lord shared this last parable with His disciples, He encouraged them in their work with the following words: "Therefore every teacher of the law who has been instructed about the kingdom of heaven is like the owner of a house who brings out of his storeroom new treasures as well as old" (Matthew 13:52).

As a backdrop, in Matthew 9:37 Jesus informed His disciples that "the harvest is plentiful but the workers are few." In Matthew 10 Jesus called His disciples to Himself and gave them authority and specific instructions in being fishers of men. We see the continued training of the disciples in Matthew 11–12. And finally, in Matthew 13, Jesus taught His disciples about heaven, hell, and the final judgment.

In Matthew 13:52 Jesus reminded the disciples that they had been instructed and trained in discipleship. They spent time with the Master learning and observing. He had prepared their hearts and nurtured their spirits. They were now like the owner or head of a house who has responsibility over others. As good stewards of what they possessed, they were to dispense from the "storeroom" of their wisdom and experience both new and old treasures.

Jesus had taught the disciples about the mysteries of life that now could be taught to others. Their understanding of both the Old and New Testaments was to be scattered out into all the world so that humankind might know and accept the Lord Jesus Christ as Savior.

I believe Jesus is asking the same questions of His disciples today. Have we really studied the Master and learned from Him? Are we trying to imitate Him in our daily living? Have we really accepted the profound and everlasting truths that transform our lives? If we know there will be a final separation of the righteous from the wicked, are we seeking to introduce others to His saving grace?

The Ideals of a Disciple

These discipleship truths have profoundly affected my life. I have therefore resolved myself to some ideals that you might consider making your own. Here they are:

• Do not take for granted your time to be an effective disciple. Life is uncertain and fragile at best. Not everyone reading this book will live to be 85 years of age and have plenty of time to evaluate life's priorities.

With every passing day, our Lord's return draws closer.

Many people need to be introduced to His saving grace. "Behold, now is the accepted time; behold, now is the day of salvation" (2 Corinthians 6:2 KJV). As you witness, try to share old truths in ever new ways and with ever new illustrations.

• Second, try to demonstrate God's grace in all you do. We are saved because someone shared with us about God's love and favor. Guard against being judgmental. Involve yourself in the world. If the disciples had just stayed with their Christian friends, we wouldn't have seen the gospel spread to "all nations."

I like the way Chuck Swindoll describes being strong in grace:

> The apostle Paul knows that few things are more winsome and refreshing than grace. It breathes life into all relationships, including discipling relationships. And Paul's encouragement to you is to be strong, literally "to be strengthened within"—let grace be reflected in your attitude.[2]

A practical way to do this is to give disciples room to grow through their failures and mistakes. "You therefore, my son, be strong in the grace that is in Christ Jesus" (2 Timothy 2:1 NASB).

• Third, I believe my best energies should be devoted to discipling my family. The lessons learned from my brain surgery taught me well about the truly important people in my life. Our first ministry field should be our family.

One of the primary reasons for the fall of Rome was the breakdown of the family. The main reason America has declined as a great nation is that we have forsaken God and the biblical family values that provided the fertile seedbed for prosperity and allegiance (see 1 Timothy 5:8).

• Fourth, we cannot invest in others without *spending time* with them. The time we spend discipling others is precious. It shows people our real concern and testifies to Christ's love in us. Our actions will always speak louder to a person being discipled than do our words.

The apostle Paul wrote to Timothy, "The things which you have heard from me in the presence of many witnesses, these entrust to faithful men, who will be able to teach others also" (2 Timothy 2:2 NASB). Paul took the time to entrust (or deposit) God's Word into Timothy's life, and now he wanted Timothy to deposit it into the lives of others. The Word that is deposited in faithful disciples is to be multiplied in the lives of many others.

• Fifth, we need to live pure lives. We should constantly be striving to model Christlikeness in our daily living. We should all join the psalmist who prayed, "Create in me a pure heart, O God, and renew a steadfast spirit within me" (Psalm 51:10).

We need to remember that God did not call us because we are holy. He called us that we might *become* holy. Holiness is the beauty produced by His workmanship.

James, the half brother of Jesus, reminded us of this objective in James 1:27: "Religion that God our Father accepts as pure and faultless is this: to look after orphans and widows in their distress and to keep oneself from being polluted by the world." I believe the widows and orphans of our day are the many, many single-parent families—involving both moms and their kids.

We need to commit ourselves to discipling the many lonely children who are the byproducts of failed marriages. Maybe Cotton Cordell has the right idea: First teach a boy to love God. Then teach him to love his family. Finally teach him to fish. And by the time he reaches his teens, no dope-peddler under the sun will ever have a chance to teach him anything.

• Sixth, discipleship requires a steadfast faith. We continually need to put our trust in Him who is able. Even our faith is a gift, "For by grace you have been saved through faith; and that not of yourselves, it is the gift of God" (Ephesians 2:8 NASB.) To overcome the challenges of the world we must *believe* that Jesus is the Son of God (1 John 5:4-5).

To be sure, we will be tested and tried. With a strong

faith, though, we can endure all things. By keeping our gaze fixed upon Jesus, we can "overcome all the power of the enemy" (Luke 10:19).

A disciple's focus should be that of the apostle Paul:

> Remember Jesus Christ, raised from the dead, descended from David. This is my gospel, for which I am suffering even to the point of being chained like a criminal. But God's word is not chained. Therefore I endure everything for the sake of the elect, that they too may obtain the salvation that is in Christ Jesus, with eternal glory. (2 Timothy 2:8-10)

And so, as we draw to a close, let us unite together with our faith in the living God to embark upon a lifelong fishing trip that is what I like to think of as "the ultimate fishing adventure." *Let's go fishing!*

Personal Growth

- Is there anything keeping you from becoming Christ's disciple?

- Would you like to dedicate or rededicate your life to Christ? If so:

  1. Admit to God that you are a sinner and are in need of a Savior.

  2. Be willing to repent of your sins.

  3. Believe that Jesus Christ died for you on the cross and rose bodily from the grave.

  4. By prayer, invite Jesus Christ to come in and take control of your life through the Holy Spirit.

  5. Get into a "fishermen's fellowship" (a church).

6. Acknowledge your decision publicly. Tell others of your new-found faith.

7. Write to me so I can support you with prayer and resources:

> Jim Grassi
> P.O. Box 434
> Moraga, CA 94556

The following poem is dedicated to all those who take the time to disciple single-parent kids.

Sammy's Wish
by Stan Fagerstrom

None of us knows what God has in mind
For you or for me, and sometimes we find
That he sends us down some unknown lane;
I know it's true because it was made very plain.

I travel a bunch and when I'm on the road
I get so darn lonesome it's like pulling a load;
And one day last fall I followed my rule
To always go for a walk and it led by a school.

I stood there awhile and watched the kids play;
As I turned to walk off I heard a voice say,
"My name is Sammy and I wanted to see
Have you got a minute you could talk to me?

My daddy got killed in that Desert Storm war;
My mother says I'll never see him no more;
I guess if I had only one special wish,
It would be for a dad who could teach me to fish."

"Now look, kid," I said, as gruff as I could,
"Don't be talkin' to strangers; I could be up to no good."
But I looked over my shoulder as I walked away;
I was hoping he'd run off with the others to play.

I went back to my room and just sat there thinking,
With a heart full of sadness and my spirits sinking;
So a couple hours later I jumped in my car
And drove back to the school; it wasn't that far.

I waited near the fence until school was done
And I watched all the kids until I spotted that one;
He'd gone maybe a mile, when he turned down a lane,
And crossed over some tracks to a small house so plain.

I walked up to that shack and knocked at the door;
The woman who answered had been sweeping the floor;
She looked up at me and said, "What do you want?"
And what I saw in her face will my dreams ever haunt.

I said, "Don't misunderstand," not knowing what to say,
"But I just ran into your Sammy today;
He told me he wanted to learn how to fish;
I'd sure like to help that little boy get his wish."

Well, she wasn't sure and it didn't surprise,
But it was easy to see the want in her eyes;
I gave her the number of some friends in that town;
I said, "Check me out, I'll be back around."

I didn't get back to that place for awhile,
But what happened when I did still makes me smile;
I'd loaded my wagon so full of tackle and gear,
That kid could fish until this time next year.

His mother ran out the door as I came up to the walk;
"Mister," she said, "you'n me gotta talk";
That's when she told me she'd been praying, you see,
That someone out there might be someone like me.

To help take the place of a dad her son wouldn't know,
I told her I'd try, but it was so hard not to show
The way my heart was pounding and my feelings inside;
I knew then who had sent me to Little Sam's side.

I stop and see Sammy every chance I get;
We fish together and I've never yet
Felt lost or lonely when his hand's in mine;
While we're together the sun seems always to shine.

His mom's found a job on the other side of town;
She told me they were moving last time I was down;
And tonight when I kneel in my motel room to pray,
I'll thank God again for sending Sammy my way.

As I said before, we don't always know
What God has in mind as we reap and we sow;
But he made my life richer, I can't measure the joy,
Just by letting me help that one little boy.[1]

Why don't you take a kid fishing!

Bibliography

Aldrich, Joseph C. *Gentle Persuasion.* Portland, OR: Multnomah Press, 1988.
_____. *Life-Style Evangelism.* Portland, OR: Multnomah Press, 1981.
_____. *Living Proof.* Colorado Springs: Navpress, 1989
Bennett, William J. *The Book of Virtues.* New York: Simon and Schuster, 1993.
Bonhoeffer, Dietrich. *The Cost of Discipleship.* New York: Macmillan Publishing Co., 1963.
Boreham, F. W. *The Uttermost Star.* London: Epworth Press, 1935.
Coleman, Robert E. *The Master Plan of Evangelism.* Grand Rapids: Fleming H. Revell, 1993.
Hull, Bill. *Jesus Christ, Disciple Maker.* Grand Rapids: Fleming H. Revell, 1990.
Jones, E. Stanley. *How to Pray.* Nashville, TN: Abingdon Press, 1979.
MacDonald, Gordon. *Ordering Your Private World.* Nashville, TN: Thomas Nelson Publishers, 1985.
_____. *Restoring Your Spiritual Passion.* Nashville, TN: Thomas Nelson Publishers, 1986.
Needham, David C. *Close to His Majesty.* Portland, OR: Multnomah Press, 1987.
Nun, Mendel. *The Sea of Galilee and Its Fishermen in the New Testament.* Ein Gev, Israel: Kibbutz Ein Gev Publishing, 1989.
Ogilvie, Lloyd J. *Making Stress Work for You.* Waco, TX: Word, 1984.
Petersen, Jim. *Lifestyle Discipleship.* Colorado Springs, CO: NavPress, 1993.
_____. *Living Proof.* Colorado Springs, CO: Navpress, 1989.
Phillips, J. B. *Your God Is Too Small.* New York: Macmillan Publishing Co., 1961.
Richards, Lawrence O. *The 365-Day Devotional Commentary.* Wheaton, IL: Victor Books, 1931.
Swindoll, Charles R. *Discipleship-Bible Study Guide.* Fullerton, CA: Insight for Living, 1990.
_____. *Laugh Again.* Waco, TX: Word, 1991.
Thayer, Joseph Henry. *Greek-English Lexicon of the New Testament.* New York: Harper Brothers Publishers, 1899.

Notes

A Personal Note from the Author
1. Dietrich Bonhoeffer, *The Cost of Discipleship* (New York: Macmillan Publishing Co., 1963), pp. 63-64.

First Catch
1. Joseph Henry Thayer, *Greek-English Lexicon of the New Testament* (New York: Harper Brothers Publishers, 1899), p. 389.
2. Bill Hull, *Jesus Christ, Disciple Maker* (Grand Rapids: Fleming H. Revell, 1990), p. 67.

Chapter 2—Priorities: Lost in the Fog
1. E. Stanley Jones, *How to Pray* (Nashville, TN: Abingdon Press, 1979), p. 5.
2. Ibid., p. 6.
3. Ibid.

Chapter 4—Concentration: The Key to Fishing Success
1. William J. Bennett, *The Book of Virtues* (New York: Simon and Schuster, 1993), p. 312.
2. Unknown author, "Footprints."
3. David C. Needham, *Close to His Majesty* (Portland, OR: Multnomah Press, 1987), pp. 13-14.

Chapter 5—Faith: A Vision for Fishing
1. Lawrence O. Richards, *The 365-Day Devotional Commentary* (Wheaton, IL: Victor Books, 1931), p. 16.
2. John H. Sammis, *"Trust and Obey"—The Hymnal for Worship and Celebration* (Waco, TX: Word Music, 1986), p. 349.

Chapter 6—Perseverance: The Patient Fisherman
1. William J. Bennett, *The Book of Virtues* (New York: Simon and Schuster, 1993), p. 529.
2. Gordon MacDonald, *Restoring Your Spiritual Passion* (Nashville, TN: Fleming H. Revell, 1986), p. 18.
3. Ibid., p. 24.

4. J. B. Phillips, *Your God Is Too Small* (New York: Macmillan, 1961), p. 56.
5. MacDonald, pp. 34-35.

Chapter 7—Proper Attitude and Equipment: The Call to Fish
1. Bill Hull, *Jesus Christ, Disciple Maker* (Grand Rapids: Fleming H. Revell, 1990), p. 71.

Chapter 8—Overcoming Obstacles: Big Bad Sharks
1. Charles R. Swindoll, *Laugh Again* (Waco, TX: Word, 1991), p. 40.

Chapter 9—Discouragement: Tough Days, Empty Livewells
1. Charles Stanley, message delivered in 1992 in Atlanta, Georgia.
2. Mendel Nun, *The Sea of Galilee and Its Fishermen in the New Testament* (Ein Gev, Israel: Kibbutz Ein Gev Publishing, 1989), pp. 28-34.

Chapter 10—Reflection: When the Tournament Is Over
1. Robert Jamieson, A. R. Fausset, and David Brown, *A Commentary*, vol. 3 (Grand Rapids: William B. Eerdmans, 1993), p. 485.

Chapter 11: Learning to Fish: The Instruction Manual
1. Ken Carpenter, *Spirit of Revival*, August 1982.

Chapter 12: Go and Make Disciples: Friendly Conversion
1. William Reinhart, *Can a Fish Forget?* (Concord, CA: 1994).
2. Joseph C. Aldrich, *Gentle Persuasion* (Portland, OR: Multnomah Press, 1988).
3. Christian Businessmen's Committee of the USA, *Lifestyle Evangelism* (Chattanooga, TN: CBMC Press, 1982), p. 5.
4. Ibid., pp. 11-12.

Chapter 13: Fishing with the Disciples: Your Net or Mine?
1. Mendel Nun, *The Sea of Galilee and Its Fishermen in the New Testament* (Ein Gev, Israel: Kibbutz Ein Gev Publishing, 1989), pp. 16-22.
2. Ibid., pp. 23-27.
3. Ibid., pp. 27-34.
4. Christian Businessmen's Committee of the USA, *Lifestyle Evangelism* (Chattanooga, TN: CBMC Press, 1982), p. 58.

Chapter 14—Drawn to the Light: Considering the Ultimate Question
1. F. W. Boreham, *The Uttermost Star* (London: Epworth Press, 1935).

Chapter 15—Fellowship: Joining a Fishing Club
1. Bill Hull, *Jesus Christ, Disciple Maker* (Grand Rapids: Fleming H. Revell, 1990), p. 10.
2. Lorne Sanny, "Fishless Fishermen," *The Equipper*, August 1994, p. 1.
3. Jim Petersen, *Lifestyle Discipleship* (Colorado Springs, CO: NavPress, 1993), pp. 152-53.

4. Hull, p. 102.
5. Joseph C. Aldrich, *Life-Style Evangelism* (Portland, OR: Multnomah Press, 1981), p. 11.
6. Robert E. Coleman, *The Master Plan of Evangelism* (Grand Rapids: Fleming H. Revell, 1993), p. 101.

Postscript—An Eternal Perspective
1. Mendel Nun, *The Sea of Galilee and Its Fishermen in the New Testament* (Ein Gev, Israel: Kibbutz Ein Gev Publishing, 1989), pp. 16-17.
2. Charles R. Swindoll, *Discipleship—Bible Study Guide* (Fullerton, CA: Insight for Living, 1990), p. 98.

Sammy's Wish
1. Stan Fagerstrom, "Sammy's Wish," *The Lure*, January 1994.

"FISHERS OF MEN" - MATTHEW 4:18-20
JESUS CHRIST CALLING PETER & ANDREW
BY *Mox Greiner Jr.* 10/15/74 ©

Other Good
Harvest House Reading

15-MINUTES ALONE WITH GOD FOR MEN
by *Bob Barnes*

A devotional that encourages men to fulfill their high calling as husbands, fathers, workers, and companions. Explores the vast riches and depths of God for men wanting to walk with Him, and not just talk about Him.

GOD'S MAN IN THE FAMILY
by *Floyd McClung*

Unrealistic expectations and burdens have made it nearly impossible for today's Christian man to keep up with his role as a husband and father. Discover the Bible's refreshingly short list.

THE FATHER HEART OF GOD
by *Floyd McClung*

The compassion of the Father enables us to overcome insecurity and the devastating effects of some of life's most painful experiences. Included in the back is a study guide with questions for each chapter.

Dear Reader,

We would appreciate hearing from you regarding this Harvest House nonfiction book. It will enable us to continue to give you the best in Christian publishing.

1. What most influenced you to purchase *Promising Waters?*
   - ❑ Author
   - ❑ Subject matter
   - ❑ Backcover copy
   - ❑ Recommendations
   - ❑ Cover/Title
   - ❑ Other_____

2. Where did you purchase this book?
   - ❑ Christian bookstore
   - ❑ General bookstore
   - ❑ Department store
   - ❑ Grocery store
   - ❑ Other_____

3. Your overall rating of this book?
   - ❑ Excellent ❑ Very good ❑ Good ❑ Fair ❑ Poor

4. How likely would you be to purchase other books by this author?
   - ❑ Very likely ❑ Not very likely ❑ Somewhat likely ❑ Not at all

5. What types of books most interest you? (Check all that apply.)
   - ❑ Women's Books
   - ❑ Marriage Books
   - ❑ Current Issues
   - ❑ Christian Living
   - ❑ Bible Studies
   - ❑ Fiction
   - ❑ Biographies
   - ❑ Children's Books
   - ❑ Youth Books
   - ❑ Other_____

6. Please check the box next to your age group.
   - ❑ Under 18 ❑ 18-24 ❑ 25-34 ❑ 35-44 ❑ 45-54 ❑ 55 and over

Mail to: Editorial Director
Harvest House Publishers
1075 Arrowsmith
Eugene, OR 97402

Name _____

Address _____

State _____ Zip _____

Thank you for helping us to help you in future publications!